T0209221

THE
PANDEMIC

TECHNOLOGY
AND THE
DEVOLUTION
OF HUMANITY

KATHRYN ROSE
AND PETER TREX

iUniverse®

THE PANDEMIC
TECHNOLOGY AND THE DEVOLUTION OF HUMANITY

iUniverse books may be ordered through booksellers or by contacting:

iUniverse
1663 Liberty Drive
Bloomington, IN 47403
www.iuniverse.com
844-349-9409

ISBN: 978-1-6632-2148-3 (sc)
ISBN: 978-1-6632-2149-0 (e)

Print information available on the last page.

iUniverse rev. date: 04/16/2021

CONTENTS

PREFACE

THE PANDEMIC HAS BEEN AN EVOLUTION OF THOUGHT WHICH HAS really developed as a journey of discovery. On our own paths to awareness, we came across different information that we needed to research for ourselves. It was necessary to get to the bottom of what was actually going on. *The Pandemic* should be a similar journey for the readers. It is meant to incite questions, to start your brain asking questions it may never have thought of asking before. The Covid-19 pandemic was a disaster on a global scale. It was the one thing that brought the entire world together, looking in one direction, putting aside religion, war, and politics. This pandemic is one of the only things that would be able to create a global community as such. Other possibilities include a natural disaster, and on a global scale, the threat of extinction from an asteroid, or visitation of life forms from somewhere other than our planet. These things create a global community that supersedes war, country, and religion. The pandemic unified the world with one focus, one vision, for the first time in our lives.

This is the starting block of awakening. The masses are looking at one thing, so attention is pulled away from all other things and is focused back on humanity. This can be both a blessing and a curse. In 2020 we were all in the same boat; all around the world there were quarantines, shutdowns, and the closing of businesses. The media had twenty-four-hour Covid-19 coverage. We lived in a fear-based society, not knowing how bad the pandemic would get or how many would be affected. We heard of the death toll rising daily as the number of cases across the world doubled, spread, and spiked out of control. We saw some of the worst of human behaviour and some of the best with sacrifices being made by frontline workers on a daily basis. The world has hit reset. Now what will we learn from the pandemic, and what will we do with that knowledge moving forward?

INTRODUCTION

W<small>E HAVE BEEN LIED TO, IN MANY DIFFERENT WAYS AND ABOUT</small> many things, but mostly about ourselves, specifically who we are, where we have come from, and what we are capable of. We've also been told the lie that life is supposed to be hard, that we are supposed to be born, go to school, get a job, and have a family and are not supposed to question our lives, our governments, or our religions. We have been told the lie that our consciousness is separate, that we can have no effect on our surroundings by willing or manifesting. We no longer recognize our potential to bring any desired experience into being. We have been conditioned with a will *not* to know. The further away we get from truth, the less we are able to tap into our abilities. We are devolving, and technology, which is supposed to be making our lives easier, is actually enhancing this process. Our reliance on computers and smartphones means we are using our brains less. We don't need to remember; we can easily look up information. We don't need to think; we have calculators to give us the answers to math problems. We don't need to develop interpersonal skills; we can hide behind computers and order our mates online from a catalogue. We are being told that humans are at the top of our development and that historically the human race was primitive, yet we see more and more proof that there were vast advanced civilizations that were interconnected across the globe. So what is the truth?

Recent events with the Covid-19 pandemic have brought the world together in a way it never has been before. It also showed us the worst side of fear with hoarding, violence, and new scams to prey on people's anxieties. As the disease continues to spread, governments and businesses around the world have undertaken unprecedented measures which are akin to wartime efforts. Countries have been put into lockdown, schools have been closed, and all events have been cancelled, with millions either told to work from home or being out of work completely. No economic cost was spared to stem the spread of the virus and support those affected by it. Countries that enacted early detection measures for the virus, quickly allocated medical resources, and issued immediate social distancing measures fared better than countries that didn't take the spread as seriously. The pandemic took over the twenty-four-hour news cycle, with broadcast media running almost nonstop coverage in many countries. Viewers, hungry to follow the up-to-date information, tracked the growing number of cases worldwide. The coronavirus has been a stress test for countries around the world, causing a devastating strain on the economy and on healthcare systems. It has shown us our world in a way we never could have imagined, where the freedoms which we took for granted were curtailed immediately and life as we knew it changed.

The one silver lining in this event was our access to technology. Imagine if we didn't have the means of global communication to be able to track the spread and react quickly. It could be said that the disease wouldn't have been able to spread in such a far-flung way if it weren't for our ability to travel globally, but our technological advances have definitely served us in our ability to staunch the explosion of cases.

So how do we define technology? The official definition from the Oxford English Dictionary is derived from the Greek word τέχνη, "the sum of techniques, skills, methods, and processes used in the production of goods or services or in the accomplishment of objectives". Technology might be the knowledge behind the techniques and processes, or it might be the physical machinery for operations without a detailed knowledge of their workings. For example, we can know how to use a computer without knowing exactly how it works. Technology involves everything from the simplest tools and their basic use; to controlling fire; to the wheel; to the Industrial Revolution; and to the cell phone and internet. Technology has helped lead to the development of the global economy. It influences the values of society and raises efficiencies in human productivity. There are disagreements over whether technology improves the human condition or worsens it, but we will get into that later. The three stages of technology are (1) tools, (2) machines, and (3) automation. It is important to look at the technological process in this way because it will relate to the later question of the necessity of technology in our lives. An economic implication of the above-mentioned idea is that intellectual labour will become increasingly more important as machines take over our physical labour.

The conflicting views on whether technology is a positive for humanity or a negative is the result of the love-hate relationship we have with it; we love the new developments but hate how fast the world is changing because of it. During the Industrial Revolution, the coal industry, the textile industry, locomotion, and the chemical industry brought the world closer together. Advances in areas of anatomy and medical science enhanced life expectancy and reduced illness. The twentieth century saw a range of technologies that evoked both awe and fear in humankind. The aeroplane, rockets, electronics, antibiotics, and nuclear power managed to create a social situation that offered security but always had danger looming on the fringes. The use and abuse of natural resources brought about rapid growth and prosperity to countries, but with such terrible side effects as pollution and depletion of resources. And as we are now well into the twenty-first century, technology has reached a whole different level. Communication as we knew it has changed and has turned passive and more indirect. Pagers, desktop computers, and telephones have now been replaced with laptops, tablets, and smartphones. On the negative side, increased use of cell phones and microwave ovens has been linked to diseases caused by radiation. Overexposure to the virtual world has created a warped sense of reality for many. We have become so attuned to communicating via social media that any face-to-face communication seems awkward. Technology today does not require us to leave our houses. One can work from home, shop from home, and receive medical care at home. This has led to isolation, a lack of social skills, and an inability to conduct ourselves in public. A strong example of this is found in a study conducted by the US Centers for Disease Control and Prevention on the mental health challenges caused by the Covid-19 pandemic, including the impact of physical distancing and stay-at-home orders. Anxiety and depressive disorders rose significantly during the months of April to June 2020, when the study was conducted, compared to the same period in 2019 in the United States. Overall, 40.9 per cent of respondents reported at least one adverse mental or behavioural health condition, including symptoms of anxiety disorder or depressive disorder (30.9%), symptoms of a trauma- and stressor-related disorder (TSRD) related to the pandemic (26.3%), and having started or increased substance use to cope with stress or emotions related to Covid-19 (13.3%). The percentage of respondents who reported having seriously considered suicide in the thirty days before completing the survey (10.7%) was significantly higher among respondents aged eighteen to twenty-four (25.5%), minority racial/ethnic groups (Hispanic respondents [18.6%] and non-Hispanic black [black] respondents [15.1%]), self-reported unpaid caregivers for adults (30.7%), and essential workers (21.7%). Community-level intervention and prevention efforts, including health communication strategies, designed to reach these groups could help address various mental health conditions associated with the Covid-19 pandemic.

Technology can also be credited with the creation of a great number of couch potatoes. Video games, YouTube, and social media are robbing us of our exercise time. Depression, stress, and poor sleep habits are increasingly becoming common medical occurrences. And, of course, privacy is an issue with phishing, viruses, and hacking—the new forms of robbery—which not only result in huge losses but also keep the perpetrator anonymous. Addiction, lack of empathy, more violence, development issues in children, lack of attention, and many more issues have been associated with technology.

One of the challenges we face is that the definition of technology only represents what humankind currently knows. It is extremely difficult to embrace or define technology that we cannot comprehend, and those who do try to do this are often ridiculed. Take for example Nikola Tesla. He himself knew he was ahead of his time. He proposed many advances in radio, television, robotics, and electricity that we use today, but he also worked on developing futuristic technologies that have yet to come to fruition, because of either the limitations of current technology or market viability. He believed in free energy accessibility for everyone but was shut down by J. P. Morgan and Morgan's investors as providing free energy is not profitable.

But did Tesla have the right idea? And was this the type of technology that our ancestors had access to? The questions we need to be asking do not look towards the future of technology as much as look at how we have gotten to where we are and why we have reached this point. Human beings in the past didn't have advanced scientific technology, but they had an ability to be completely at one with planet. This was their technology, which we no longer have access to—one of the main reasons we cannot figure out how many of the great works of civilization were accomplished. We simply cannot fathom a technology not based in science or the use of tools.

We have lost our ability to connect with the natural energies of the planet to power our lives and societies. One law of thermodynamics states that energy cannot be created or destroyed, only changed in form. Perhaps the loss of connection with the natural energies is causing an impact on a global scale that we haven't even considered yet. In a leap from physics to culture, hard science is being applied to social science with principles that need to be understood through basic biology. If the scientific laws of biology are not static as we continue to learn, might it be possible that the laws of thermodynamics may also be in flux? Can we use the laws that we do know of to quantify social change? Can we explain our near past, our current state, and even our history through entropy? If we look at technology and advancements as a social tool, then what do we think happens to social energy with the stimulus of overinformation, misinformation, or disinformation? As the government damages the credibility of the media and vice versa, what happens to society? What about our infrastructure?

We as living beings are open systems, exchanging both matter and energy with our environment. We take in food and oxygen from our surroundings, exchanging it for internal energy and a release of carbon dioxide. In the same way that this law applies to us, every living thing on the planet and, in fact, the universe itself follows these rules (within our understanding). Focusing on the first and second laws of thermodynamics, we have used technology and science to change the types of energy we are using and expending. The degree of randomness or disorder in a system is called entropy. Since we know that every energy transfer results in the conversion of some energy to an unusable form (such as heat), and since heat that does not do work goes towards increasing the randomness of the universe, we can state that humans are actually causing entropy without returning useful energy to the planet. The net effect of the original process (local decrease in entropy) and the energy transfer (increase in entropy of surroundings) is an overall increase in the entropy of the universe. To sum up, our increasing population of the planet is maintained by a constant input of energy and is offset by an increase in the entropy of our surroundings. Energy can never be destroyed, but what it can do is change from more-useful forms to less-useful forms. Are we now using less-useful forms of energy because we have forgotten how to access higher forms? Does the fact that we are pillaging the resources of the planet instead of living in harmony with the energy frequencies mean we have disrupted the entire energy of the planet? If we are not tapping into and using the energy, then where is it going and what is it being used for? Are we left with higher levels of heat at the earth's core? If heat is not doing work, it increases the randomness (or disorder) of the universe. What is the earth doing with the additional heat, and how will that affect us? What was the purpose behind our change in energy use? Was it for profit, power, or something else? Were we forced into this change? What was the impact of that?

The universe is not only expanding but also getting faster as it inflates. If we look at the Bing Bang theory as the explanation of the cycle we are currently in, we should also look at the theory proposing that this has happened before. Think of the universe as an elastic band that is in the process of stretching out. Once it reaches an unknown outer level of expansion, will it start the cycle over to compress until the pressure is so great that it explodes outwards again? Is this the natural process by which energy is generated again and again? If the cosmos is going through a regular cycle of inflation and deflation, does this give us a plausible understanding of all creation and destruction? Absolutes don't exist; even gravity can be anything anywhere—and we only know how it works for us and our planet right now. Humanity thrives on the premise that order prevails as a result of deliberate intentions and that we are the controllers of order as such. However, order predates human existence and one does not mess with Mother Nature. Organized chaos recognizes the fact that most organisms, including human beings, thrive when they can set their own norms, not by written law but by unspoken law. If organized chaos is the natural ebb and flow, we must consider that human evolution and devolution has no impact on the outcome of cosmic survival. We are taking a journey that the planet has gone through countless times.

If our evolution has no effect on what happens to the planet, then why are we constantly looking for answers to life and creation outside our world? There is the possibility of as many worlds and planets with life as there are grains of sand on the beach. We cannot find life forms any but on our planet yet because we are only looking for grains of sand on our beach … Just how many beaches are there out there? Why are we looking for life outside ourselves and our own history without even understanding who we are and where we came from? We only focus on the unknowns in our future, not looking for answers to enable an understanding of our past. We brush off the unknown with a shrug and a nod to unknown external influences. What if everything we have found is us, our own history and past that is so unknown? Perhaps the why is what we should be digging into for our own foundation of human evolution. We need not to be so limited in our use of the word *technology* as the word is only defined as it applies to us directly. Just as we can only understand gravity as it applies to us, we can only see technology as tools. This may be the most limiting factor in our evolution, our inability to understand our own past and our rigid definitions of technology. Current technology in this decade is defined by quantum computers, smartphone technology, and development of space exploration capabilities. A century ago, there was no computing technology, the automobile was new, and we defined technology based on our industrial advancements. Two centuries ago, we were powered by coal and had no global communication. Technological advancements are tying the world together as one community, one resource, but where is this taking us?

The Pandemic is about questioning the truth that we have been told as a species about where we were, where we are, and where we are going as a global society. It is a journey of discovery following a road map of historical clues indicating that something is not right. We haven't been told the entire story. There are too many clues and inconsistencies in our archaeology and sciences, our religion and politics. Knowledge that was long hidden is being rediscovered. We live in the age of computers, where space travel happened decades ago. We are exploring the universe in greater depths than ever before. We have a rover on Mars. Scientists are discovering black holes, and string theory is becoming more plausible. The question of whether we are alone is less and less likely answered with a yes as we discover worlds that can support life. We must look at the clues we are given as a whole, questioning the status quo and expanding our awareness on the journey towards answers. *The Pandemic* is not about those answers, but rather poses important questions for our society to begin examining in greater depth.

Let's go back to the beginning.

CHAPTER 1

Ancient Architecture

A S A SOCIETY, WE BELIEVE THAT WE ARE AT THE PEAK OF OUR evolution at this current point in human history. Our advances in science and technology seem to support this progressive point of view. We are not talking about humans evolving from apes. Even Charles Darwin never claimed that humankind was descended from the apes, but rather from theoretical common ancestors which were a node for the divergence of species into separate lineages. This "missing link" was never identified with certainty as fossil relationships are unclear, even within the more recent *Homo sapiens* lineage. What we have been told by Darwin is that we are evolving. So, what is evolution? Darwin's general theory presumes the development of life from nonlife and stresses a purely naturalistic (undirected) "descent with modification". That is, complex creatures evolve from more simplistic ancestors naturally over time. As random genetic mutations occur within an organism's genetic code, the beneficial mutations are preserved because they aid in survival, a process better known as "natural selection". These beneficial mutations are passed on to the next generation, and over time they accumulate. The result is an entirely different organism (not just a variation of the original, but an entirely different creature). Darwin's theory has been proven incorrect, or at least incomplete. His critics challenged that if the theory of natural selection of Darwin were correct, we should be able to see the intermediate forms of species, the connecting links—which was not the case. Darwin did not have the answer, nor the archaeological evidence to back up his theory, but we still use the idea of progression in culture and society as if it were a known

1

entity. The message of Darwin's *On the Origin of the Species* is that humans and other animals are part of an evolutionary continuum, an evolutionary inevitability.

Conversely, devolution is the notion that species can revert to more primitive forms over time. It is based on a presumption that evolution has a purposeful direction towards increasing complexity and therefore there can be an opposite idea of a decay in complexity. The concept of devolution as regress from progress relates to the ancient idea that humans are the ultimate product of all universal existence. From a biological perspective, there is no such thing as devolution, as all changes in gene frequencies in populations are by definition evolutionary changes. Each change is not related to an adaptation to the environment around us—the amount of hair on our bodies, the number of fingers we have, the number of toes we have for upright walking, eyelids, etc.—but rather each population contains a variant of traits that are passed along based on dominancy and the regressive tendencies of our genetics. Nonetheless, many people evaluate nonhuman organisms according to human standards of anatomy and physiology and mistakenly conclude that humans are the ultimate product of evolution. But are we? If we are at the height of human existence, then why is there still so much that we don't know about our own past? There are amazing feats that were achieved by ancient civilizations that we cannot explain with our modern engineering. We have created stories and explanations about how things were done by "primitive" people with the limited tools we assume they must have had. The reason that stories about the advanced technology of ancient civilizations that have collapsed are so appealing is because of the genuine mysteries presented by our distant past. There seems to be an almost universal suspicion that things were once much better. We have all heard the term "the good old days", referring to a time when things were assumed to be simpler and with less complication. This attitude is embedded in myths of the golden age and in tales of Atlantis and other lost paradises. We create explanations of understanding to fill these holes when we cannot find a solution that fits.

Contrary to our current beliefs about them, ancient civilizations across the globe were highly advanced and capable of spectacular engineering accomplishments. These societies, for that is what they were, built wonders that have lasted thousands of years—roads, aqueduct systems, giant structures we can only marvel at and couldn't duplicate. Most of their structures are in ruins or have been rebuilt based on what we think we know of them, but we can only guess their purpose and what they must have looked like when newly constructed.

Monolithic Structures

I will explore several different structures that have stumped modern-day engineers. The first of these is called monolithic structures. As the name suggests, they are carved out of one large rock that can weigh hundreds of tons and stand straight up. We find a lot of these structures in the ancient Egyptian empire and refer to them as obelisks. They were erected to honour major events such as a coronation or victory in war, or to honour their gods. The Obelisk of Senusret I is one of the oldest surviving obelisks in its original location. The Romans moved many obelisks out of Egypt; in fact, there are more Egyptian obelisks around the world than there are left in Egypt today. Located still in Heliopolis, the Obelisk of Senusret I was a symbol of the sun god Ra and is thought to relate to the zodiacal light of sunrise and sunset. In the area where the obelisk stands, red granite was often used for production, but there are still many unanswered questions about these obelisks. How were the ancients able to carve the stones and then transport them and lift them without breaking them? Modern-day obelisks are not able to be constructed from single stones, and their construction demands modern tools and machinery that we cannot fathom the ancients had access to. There is a region in northern Egypt called Aswan that is known for its historical stone quarries. Here we find the Unfinished Obelisk.

At forty-two metres in height and weighing nearly twelve hundred tons, it was one of the largest obelisks created in ancient times. The project was abandoned because cracks appeared in the stone, which can still be seen in the bedrock from which it was being carved. It is thought that this would have been the companion of the Lateran Obelisk at Karnak. This monument offers us rare insight into the stoneworking techniques the ancient builders must have used. There are tool marks still visible, as well as marking lines for the outline of the obelisk. We are still guessing, but it gets us closer to understanding what the ancients were capable of.

Standing Stones

Another type of stone structure whose purpose leaves us questioning are giant standing stones. Standing stones, or menhirs, are stones set into the ground vertically. There may be single stones, circles of stones, or lines or groups of stones. The dates of these structures range mostly from 4000 BC to 1500 BC, but many have been found that are even older. They can be found across Europe, Africa, and Asia, with the greatest collection being in western Europe. The standing stones of both Easter Island and Stonehenge have baffled archaeologists as to their purpose and how they were moved. Stonehenge is in Wiltshire, England, whereas Easter Island is a Chilean island in the south-eastern Pacific Ocean. How vastly different peoples on different sides of the world had the same technology to move these stones and stand them up is inconceivable.

Stonehenge's standing stones are around thirteen feet high and seven feet wide and weigh about twenty-five tons. The stones are set within earthworks. It is believed by archaeologists that these are vast burial grounds that date to as early as 3000 BC, some believed to be much older. Similarly, the standing stones at Carnac contain burial mounds, tombs, and menhirs (single standing stones), along with groupings in alignments and rows whose purpose is still guessed at. The stones date from about 4500 BC, with a myth that the lines are the invading Roman armies turned to stone by the mage Merlin. Another location, called the Armenian Stonehenge, contains a ring of menhirs pierced with holes believed to have been used for prehistoric astronomical observation.

Easter Island's statues are called moai, created by the early Rapa Nui people. They have been dated to a period between AD 1100 and AD 1680, and they were carved with hand chisels out of solidified volcanic ash. Not only are these still standing upright, but also they have been carved with faces and placed on plinths. Like most large monuments, these, archaeologists believe, were transported using ropes to tug and rock them into place. It has been suggested that these stones were placed to face the direction of water, a precious resource. But the reasons behind their creation and why they were important to the people of the island is a mystery.

Not only did ancient civilizations have the ability to do incredible stonework, but also they built entire cities that we have found evidence of. Using lidar laser technology, researchers in Guatemala have discovered more than sixty-one thousand ancient Mayan structures. Scientists are discovering evidence of vast civilizations in the Amazon. Satellite technology has shown evidence of ruins across Syria and the Middle East, and evidence of an entire unknown race has been found under the ice in Antarctica. Another example of an extremely advanced ancient civilization is the lost city of Mohenjo-daro, located in Sindh, Pakistan. One of the most prominent urban centres in the area, it has been dated to around 2500 BC, with an estimated thirty-five thousand inhabitants. There are advanced water and sewer systems with almost every home having an indoor bathing area and drainage. There are several examples of advanced aqueduct and indoor plumbing systems in ancient societies, including in the former Roman Empire, where they could get the water to run uphill in the aqueducts and travel across long distances. More modern sewage systems, as recent as the late nineteenth century, were still so inadequate that waterborne diseases and sewage disposal were major issues for industrializing societies. Yet the technology seems to have been readily available for managing water and waste before that. What happened in our history to eradicate that knowledge?

Saksaywaman

One of the most puzzling engineering feats of ancient architects is their ability to have precision cut massive stone blocks and placed them so close together that you can't get a piece of paper between them—and the blocks are maintained without the use of mortar. A great example of this technique is the stone fortress of Saksaywaman. Situated at an altitude of twelve thousand feet, the complex is believed to have been an important religious or military location of the Incan peoples.

The boulders were excavated from a quarry that was three kilometres away and were then moved to the building site by an unknown system. What kind of tools did the Inca use to be able to cut these rocks with such precision? The boulders are huge, with the largest weighing as much as two hundred tons. How did the Incas move them? It is hypothesized that they tied ropes to the blocks and pulled them over the area. The standard explanation for the fitting of the stones without mortar is that the builders individually lifted them, checked the seams, and recarved them to fit precisely into location. However, considering the precision of the cuts and the weight of the blocks, this seems unlikely. The Incas themselves acknowledged to the Spanish conquistadores that the structures were standing long before that period and that the area had been used by different peoples. Was there another civilization that we have no record of that was more advanced than the Incas? The Incas themselves built an aqueduct and road system that connected the Inca Empire. These were very advanced people, not primitives as we have supposed. We cannot fathom the advanced techniques they must have used. However, one legend speaks of a liquid derived from plants which the ancients used to turn stones soft, after which the stones were able to reharden in particular shapes, at which point they could be set without mortar. This idea is not so different from our ability to add water to mix concrete and have it form into any shape. One thing is for sure, these ancient civilizations were more able than we have given them credit for.

Underwater Cities

Another point of evidence suggesting vastly advanced unknown societies is the many underwater cities found all over the world. There are more than two hundred sites just in the Mediterranean, with some locations showing advanced civilizations dating back more than ten thousand years, when we are told there were not supposed to be people who built vast cities. We have all heard the legend of the city of Atlantis. Even Plato wrote about the city in 360 BC— and it was thought to be from a time nine thousand years prior to his period on earth. While we have not yet found proof of Atlantis, though many have looked, we have found many other locations that have been identified.

The first of these locations is the ancient city of Dwarka, India, which, according to folklore, was the home of Lord Krishna. The ruins were found beneath the modern-day city of Dwarka, 131 feet below the ocean surface. The complexities found in this city have baffled experts. Similarly, the underwater Pyramids of Yonaguni Jima, in Japan, are baffling in terms of their construction and location. Experts have argued whether the pyramids are man-made or are a naturally occurring phenomenon. If they are man-made, they have been dated to the most recent ice age, around 10000 BC. The pyramids resemble the structures built in Mexico and Central America, but there are no other structures like them in the area.

In Greece there is a city that sank more than five thousand years ago that no one knows the history of. It is believed to have been destroyed by an earthquake and to be part of the Minoan dynasty. This seems to be one of the many cities destroyed in the area by earthquakes. A much more recent example of a city that was sunk by earthquake is the seventeenth-century Port Royal in the Caribbean, which was known as a hotbed for pirates like Blackbeard. If our recent history gives us such a strong example of what can happen to a city hit by an earthquake, how much more likely is the possibility that we have experienced many such devastating destructions over our lengthy human history?

The Sphinx

Another mystery, and great work of architecture, is the Sphinx. The Great Sphinx of Giza is a limestone statue of a mythical creature possessing the body of a lion and the head of a human. Facing directly from west to east, it stands on the west bank of the Nile. Cut from the bedrock, its original shape has been restored with layers of blocks.

It is the oldest-known sculpture, with a lot of theories of exactly how old it is, who made it, and what its purpose was. Buried for most of its life in the desert sand, the Sphinx is a mystery that is yet to be solved. A small temple between its paws contained dozens of inscribed stelae placed by the pharaohs to honour the sun god. The head is disproportionate to the size of the body; the Sphinx may have been recarved from its original form.

In terms of dating of the Sphinx, there has been plenty of debate as to its age. Some scholars have noted that the weathering patterns are consistent with water erosion rather than wind or sand. These patterns are unique to the Sphinx and are not found on any other structures in the area, leading to the conclusion that the Sphinx is much older than any other existing structure. Today Egypt is dry and arid, although it is thought that ten thousand years ago it was wet and rainy in the area.

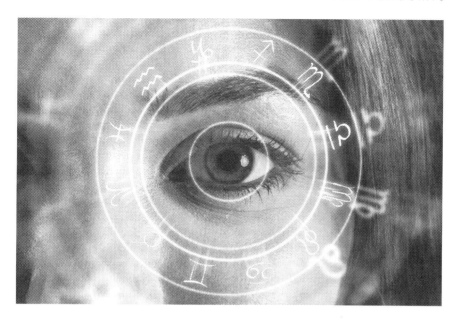

Another school of thought has it that the Great Sphinx may have been built to represent and honour the cycle of Leo, which would put its date of creation at 11600 BC. With the weathering patterns, it has been postulated that the Sphinx may be even older than we think, dating back to the previous cycle of Leo. Current restoration projects and the level of deterioration make it difficult to do any further research on the Sphinx, and preservation is at the forefront.

Pyramids

No list of ancient engineering feats would be complete without a mention of the pyramids. There are pyramids located around the world in strategic locations, the most famous of these being in Egypt. The Pyramid of Djoser, the oldest of the pyramids, is estimated to have been built around the year 2630 BC, yet it may be older than that. Still today, experts have not been able to come up with a solid conclusion to explain how the ancient Egyptians built these perfectly aligned buildings using nothing but supposed physical strength. It is presumed that as many as one hundred thousand slaves worked over the years to build these immense mysterious buildings, but could this possibly be true? Would it not make more sense that the ancient civilizations had technology that we are unaware of?

Modern architects still cannot agree on the function of pyramids. It has been speculated that the Great Pyramid was anything from a beacon for landing spacecraft, to a royal disaster shelter, to a gigantic water pump. But mainstream Egyptologists have always insisted that the Great Pyramid is a royal tomb—just a tomb, and nothing but a tomb—even though no traces of any bodies, coffins, or grave goods have ever been found in it. Not only that, but also there are no inscriptions on any of the pyramids, unlike later, smaller pyramids used as tombs, which are covered with inscriptions.

Modern archaeologists are astounded at the mathematical precision with which these buildings are aligned with stars, the sun's solstices, and the points of the compass. There are mysterious sealed internal shafts that seem to indicate stellar alignments with the Belt stars from the time it was believed to have been built, some four thousand years ago, but also from when some theorize it was first laid out twelve thousand years ago. Pyramid structures are scattered across the globe with locations in Asia, Europe, Africa, North America, and South America. They have similar shapes, construction techniques, and mathematical precision aligned to celestial events.

Besides Egypt, Teotihuacan in Mexico is home to some of the largest pyramid-like structures in the world. These are built on a site, inhabited around 100 BC, believed to have been an urban metropolis spanning twenty-two miles which was home to approximately two hundred thousand inhabitants. The city itself was built so that its grid aligned with key geographic, geodetic, and celestial points that were considered important to the society. For instance, the city's east–west axis was aligned with the sunset point on the horizon that coincided with the beginning of the Mesoamerican calendar. Also, the city's north–south axis was aligned with the Temple of Quetzalcoatl, as well as with the Sun Pyramid and the Moon Pyramid. How did these supposedly primitive people have the mathematical ability to calculate these alignments so precisely? Where did this knowledge disappear to?

Göbekli Tepe

An archaeological site in the south-eastern Anatolia region of Turkey called Göbekli Tepe is another mysterious site. We have no record of who built it, exactly when it was built, or where these people went.

Circles of massive T-shaped stone pillars were erected—the world's oldest-known megaliths. There are more than two hundred pillars in about twenty circles with a height of up to twenty feet and weighing up to ten tons each. They are fitted into sockets that were hewn out of bedrock with unknown tools. The function of these stones remains a mystery. Like the obelisks in Egypt, there are three T-shaped pillars that are unfinished, not yet having been fully carved out of the bedrock. These mammoth blocks were twenty-three feet long and ten feet wide, weighing as much as fifty tons. The slabs would have been transported more than three hundred and thirty feet from the hilltop where they were placed. Archaeologists estimate that as many as five hundred people were required to move them as this was a period prior to the invention of the modern wheel. Historians believe workers used flint points to cut these massive blocks out of the limestone, but how were they able to create such precise lines? Many of these pillars are decorated with pictures and animals, believed to be sacred to the creators. How were the people able to carve so deeply and so beautifully? If these people were not evolved, then why was decoration and art even a part of their lives?

We are lucky enough to have this hard evidence showing these engineering marvels. Clearly the knowledge existed to create these solutions. The question we need to ask is, what happened to this knowledge? Today we cut with lasers and diamond-tip saw blades. We use machines instead of manpower. In this case, has our knowledge simply evolved instead of disappearing? If so, then why can we not retrace our progression in innovation? Why does history tell us that these feats should not have been possible?

CHAPTER 2

Ancient Technology

JUST AS WE HAVE BEEN FORTUNATE TO DISCOVER ADVANCED architectural sites all over the world, there is more evidence being discovered of ancient technological advancements. We often assume ancient civilizations did not have the technology or sophistication that we do. Yet surviving to this day are several hard pieces of evidence, and in some cases the objects themselves, that show us that ancient people did indeed have a sophistication much greater than we can imagine. This is important as it shows an ability far beyond what history has attributed to our ancestors, without the use of modern-day technology. These ancient technologies prove that there was a wealth of knowledge on a global scale that we no longer have access to. Ancient peoples knew more about astronomy, our position in the greater universe, and measuring time than we do. In fact, we are still figuring these things out.

Piri Reis Map

One of the most recently made of these technological wonders was made famous in 1513 by Ottoman admiral and cartographer Piri Reis. His map first attracted attention because of the claim that it combined Christopher Columbus's data with information from ancient sources. Columbus led the first European expeditions to "discover" the Americas and the Caribbean, an area not then known to Europe, even with historical evidence of previous visitations. Approximately one-third of the Piri Reis map survives. It shows the western coast of Europe/North Africa and the eastern coast of Brazil with amazing accuracy for the time.

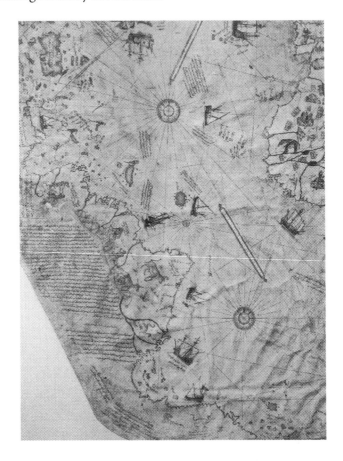

Piri used ten Arabic sources and four Indian maps sourced from the Portuguese. The map shows islands of the Caribbean, but also Antarctica, which is not known to have been seen until 1820. The coastline of the southernmost continent, claimed by Professor Charles Hapgood in his 1966 book *Maps of the Ancient Sea Kings*, was not present information Piri would have had in the 1500s. Rather, the Piri map shows this region as it was fifteen thousand years ago, before it was covered in ice. Moreover, the US Air Force determined that the base projection of the map was from a location thousands of miles directly above the Great Pyramid of Egypt. Professor Hapgood considered the Piri Reis map—and other early modern maps with anomalous geographical information—as survivals from some unknown ancient civilization that once mapped the entire planet by air or space. Who were these ancient civilizations with the capability to do this type of advanced mapping? Were they capable of air travel or even space travel, the latter being unknown to us still today?

Antikythera Computer

At the turn of the twentieth century, green lumps of corroded bronze were recovered from the wreck of a treasure ship off Antikythera Island in the Aegean. The "Antikythera mechanism" turned out to be several fused masses of gears from what was decided to be a portable astronomical computer. The mechanism is dated to the early first century, centuries before anything even close to that complex was invented in Europe.

It is thought the device was a creation of Athenian technology intended for Julius Caesar and that it was lost when the ship sank on the way to Rome. Dates could be inputted and progressed by turning a hand crank or knob. The device calculated the positions of the sun and the moon, the lunar phases, a point in several eclipse cycles, the Olympic date, and possibly planetary alignment on several dials on both the front and back panels. There were even instructions engraved on doors of the mechanism. Archaeologists have used current mechanical reconstructions and X-ray machines to discover how it was used. New capabilities continue to be found. Who created this advanced device? Where is the record of this level of sophistication in Greece?

Baghdad Battery

In 1940, a German archaeologist going through an inventory of items from a previous excavation found a terracotta pot covered in tar. He noticed that it contained a cylinder made of rolled copper and a corroded iron rod. At the top, the iron rod is isolated from the copper by bitumen, with plugs or stoppers, and both rod and cylinder fit snugly inside the opening of the jar. The copper cylinder is not watertight, so if the jar were filled with a liquid, this would surround the iron rod as well.

The artefact had been exposed to the weather and suffered corrosion. The German archaeologist hypothesized that all it needed was the addition of an acidic electrolyte such as vinegar or lemon juice to create an electrical battery. The tar was the insulator that the battery needed to work. The device is dated to the early third century, centuries before another battery was created. No other examples of this type of technology have been found, so an alternative hypothesis was suggested that it may have been used for preserving papyrus texts. We are struggling to understand a system that simply does not fit into our definition of technology.

Nineveh Telescope

Ancient Babylonian texts of two and a half millennia ago describe Saturn as having ears like a jug and a few of its moons. Jupiter's moons, which are first recorded as being seen by Galileo Galilei, were also known. Without a telescope, it would be impossible even for the keenest-sighted priest to see these things. The oldest lens in the world found in context is in the British Museum. Called the "Nineveh lens", this three-thousand-year-old faceted piece of rock crystal was discovered in the palace of Sargon II. There are older lenses in the Louvre and the Egyptian Museum in Cairo dating as far back as forty-five hundred years ago, but the Nineveh lens is the first to be considered as part of a telescope.

Ancients understood the properties of light and how lenses could be used to see far distances or accentuate extremely fine detail. Lenses in excellent condition have been found in Crete, and the Roman authors Pliny and Seneca refer to one used by an engraver in Pompeii. Lenses were used as proper magnifying glasses to do fine carvings on gems from antiquity. The Vikings, six hundred years before the official invention of the telescope, had elliptical lenses created on a lathe. The Vikings were great explorers who were more advanced in their theories, god myths, and technology than most of their contemporaries in Europe. Where did this knowledge come from?

Global Measurements

It was the collaborative effort of forty-eight nations of the world, with France leading the team, that resulted in the metrification of the measurement system around the world. The metric system is far simpler and more efficient than the imperial system of measurement. Many systems of measurement exist whose origins are lost in the dim mists of prehistory. The division of the circle into three hundred and sixty degrees, the day with twenty-four hours, and so forth all come from ancient Mesopotamia and Egypt. But even the modern English and metric systems may have roots far deeper than we have been led to believe. In Scotland and Northern Europe are circles of standing stones. Despite all their different layouts, they are all based on the same unit of measurement, termed the "megalithic yard", with a length of 2.72 feet. There is so little difference in the dimensions that it had to be derived by observing the sky at each site. It is believed that this is an ancient universal standard of measurement based on physical properties of earth, like the modern metric system. Many other units of measurement have been found to be identical as those used in the ancient world. For example, an English/imperial inch is virtually identical to the pyramid inch, which is 1.00106 inches. Another example is the measuring system in ancient Sumerian dealing with volume based on a sphere, from which the metric system is derived. What this points to is a civilization with knowledge greater than our own that we have lost. We may not be a young, undeveloped civilization as we thought, but rather a race struggling to recover information that was widely available in the past. This puts ancient technology into a different light.

Ancient Calendar

The Mayan calendar is extremely accurate and almost too precise to have been invented by a people whom we believe to be a primitive culture. The calendar is an intricate system of cycles within cycles, intermeshing like gears. These cycles are based on the sun and moon, but also on Venus, and the calendar can function flawlessly for millions of years in either direction. Most other systems for tracking time can only be used as a rough estimate for astronomical phenomena, but the Mayan system is extremely advanced and interweaves timeline and astronomy with ease.

Along one edge there is a row of seven glyphs which represent heavenly bodies and planets in the contemporary days of the week: Sun, Moon, Mars, Mercury, Jupiter, Venus, and Saturn. Days of the week were not used by the Maya that we know of, so where did this knowledge come from? Regardless of where it came from, there is no denying that humanity has had peaks of technological innovation that seem to have disappeared, as these examples show. We have to ask ourselves what these people really knew, if we know it also, and, given that it disappeared once, will it disappear again?

CHAPTER 3
Mayan Calendar and 2012

Historical stories note two main societies for their highly advanced knowledge and practices. The first of these is Atlantis, written about in Plato's works, which we have been told was destroyed. As we have not been able to find the location or any remains, the city and people have become myth and legend. But what if science fiction is indeed scientific fact? The second of these societies is the Maya. Whether what we know about them is fact or fiction, what we do have is the remains of their great nation and artefacts such as the Mayan calendar.

The date 21 December 2012 is infamous as it was believed by many to be the end of the world. People stockpiled food for the coming apocalypse, which they said was predicted by the ending of the Mayan calendar. We were at the end date of the last 5,125-year cycle, with various astronomical cataclysms being cited as the cause of the end of the world. Professional Maya scholars, however, stated that the idea of doom at the end of 2012 was a misrepresentation of Maya history and culture. December 2012 marked the conclusion of a *b'ak'tun*, or a time period used in the Mesoamerican Long Count calendar.

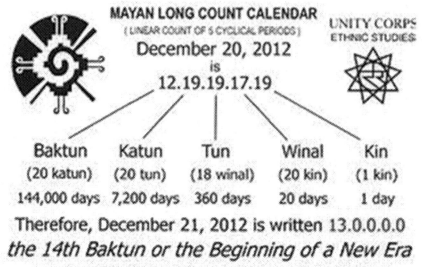

There is a strong tradition of "world ages" in Mayan literature in which there is a cycle of failed worlds, followed by a successful fourth world in which we were now living. The previous world ended after thirteen b'ak'tuns (13 × 144,000 days) ago, and the "zero date" has been set at a point which corresponds to 11 August 3114 BC. This means that our current world reached the end of its thirteenth b'ak'tun on Maya date 13.0.0.0.0, or 21 December 2012 in the Gregorian calendar. The repetition or rollover of the dates was key to the assumption the world would end.

However, the charts were not tracking apocalyptical devastation. The Mayan calendar is unique in that it charts the changing spiritual energies of cosmic evolution. Unlike many other astrological systems, it is not based on Earth's procession and the position of the stars. Its timeline dwarfs any currently used by modern astronomers as there are references to times that stretch back billions of years, much more complex and involved than anything else we find. The interval was significant in Mayan theology, but not because it spelt destruction. None of the other ruins of the Maya culture, such as the tablets and carvings that have been found, foretell the end of the world. Many Maya believed that their gods who created the world in the last age would return, set everything in order, and regenerate the cosmos. The world would be renewed, not destroyed. It would be coming out of a period of evolutionary darkness into a new world age of enlightenment. Moving through this period of change with resistance or acceptance would determine whether the transition would happen with cataclysmic changes or gradual increases of peace and tranquillity: a new golden age when humans would be heading towards a slow transformation of consciousness and moving to a higher awareness. This is what is referred to as an Omega point in time, a time of spiritual awakening, when the spirit has fully descended into matter and it is time for the spirit to rise again.

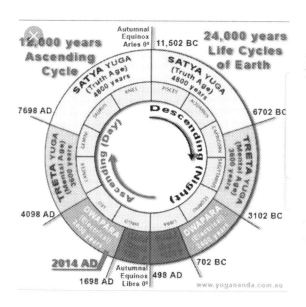

In the 1940s, Pierre Teilhard de Chardin described the Omega point as a maximum level of complexity and consciousness that the universe seems to be evolving into. It only makes sense then that the descending periods are a movement away from higher consciousness and awareness. This idea of a cyclical period is shown over and over in nature: the seasons, the birth/death cycle, and the nutrient and water cycles. Most important for humans and our existence is the carbon cycle. We breathe in oxygen and breathe out carbon dioxide, which is in conjunction with a plant's cycle of breathing in carbon dioxide and producing oxygen. Climate cycles take us through periods of ice ages to periods of global warming. Planetary cycles and the moon's cycles are obvious in the night sky. Time itself is a cycle, which makes sense as we understand everything from mathematics to music in cycles.

When delving deeper into the cycles presented by the Maya, we start with the first wave of physical matter. The next level is living cells, followed by multicellular organisms. We compound that further with family groups, tribes, and nations, then the whole of human awareness on the planet. But is that where life stops? The cycle of awareness should bring us past our own solar system to the awareness of galaxies and, beyond those, the cosmos.

The Maya integrated their calendar stages into their architecture. We see an example in Chichén Itzá, where the nine steps represent the different cycles in evolution. Each step is twenty times smaller than the last, each of the nine creation cycles being twenty times shorter than the previous cycle. The cycles are then further divided into thirteen equal sections of time, with each having its own purpose in the cycle of evolution. There are seven sections of day and six sections of night on each level. The ancient Sumerians and Mesopotamians wrote this same pattern on clay tablets as their understanding of creation. Ancient Vedic texts (the basis of Buddhism, Hinduism, Sufism, and Taoism) have the same nine levels with thirteen sections in each. Even the Judeo-Christian Bible states that there are seven days of creation in the book of Genesis. There is some discrepancy in translations of the Mayan calendar as to exactly what the last day of the cycle was. Was it 10 February 2011; was it 28 October 2011; or was it in fact 21 December 2012? The challenge seems to lie in the differences between modern-day calendars and the period shift that they contain versus the original Mayan calculations. Whatever the exact date is, we should be reaching a point of collective human consciousness at the peak of the pyramid shown in the image above.

We as a species should be making a new start, but we are not at a place to follow the path laid out in the Mayan cycle. We are barely within reach of the cycle of awareness of what it means to be human. The idea of what makes up a family group is in question, much less what makes up tribes and nations! Do we even really understand ourselves as multicellular organisms? Why are cancers destroying us then? We have seen proof over the last several thousand years of tools and technologies that divide us. Humanity has been constantly divided by wars, disease, oppression of the weak, resources, knowledge ... But from the Mayan perspective, we will come out of this dark period of repressed levels of awareness.

Religion and spirituality in recent history have been used as a reason for severe aggression against one another. In many different religions we find prophets emerging amid times of significant change as defined by the Mayan calendar. Buddha (Siddhartha Gautama) and the rise of Christianity both coincided with significant points of change. Some prophets find their message is well-received, whereas others are persecuted, and it is not until much later that their message is understood by people who have evolved enough to be open to enlightenment.

The date 21 December 2012 marked the end of a dark period for human awareness. We will emerge from that period with compassion and understanding on a global level. We see some evidence of this in the archaeological evidence left by historical builders with the same knowledge around the world. We live in a cyclical and holographic universe: our microcosms reflect the macrocosm and vice versa. Most will not recognize the evolution of consciousness, but those who seek it and embrace it will grow in understanding of our inherent purpose. So, what makes the clues in the Mayan calendar so vital to us today? Well, in general, we have in the Mayan calendar a road map of time and history. It's not a crystal ball showing the exact future in store, but it does show landmarks that prove we are on the right path as we move forward.

The Maya and the Atlanteans were both given a vast number of details on how the galactic and universal cycles work (cycles of time). As we see from the Mayan calendar, these are highly accurate relationships to the sun, stars, and equinoxes. When an end of a cycle is reached, the planet is supposed to regenerate, entering into a higher vibrational state. The Maya used the information they were given by creating things with the positive vibration. Did the Atlanteans opt for the negative? Did they rely so heavily on their advanced technology that they destroyed themselves?

CHAPTER 4

Was Our Knowledge Destroyed on Purpose?

I N EARLIER CHAPTERS I HAVE PRESENTED SPECIFIC CASES THAT baffle our current understanding. Now I will suggest that we have had our knowledge base specifically culled and that much of our history is a blur because of it. There is a range of theories behind this, involving either the Illuminati, a secret society directing the general population, the church, the cabal, politics, or some other organization. There is so much about our own history we do not know. But what we don't know is why we don't know it. Why have we been kept in the dark? Is our lack of knowledge a mistake? Have we misinterpreted the information we know about our own past in such a way that the truth has been lost? Or were we deliberately led down a wrong path, one where the narrative has been controlled and questions are discouraged?

Phantom Time Theory

Of the many theories that exist, the first I want to touch on is the phantom time hypothesis. This is a historical conspiracy theory presented by Heribert Illig, the conspiracy being that the Holy Roman emperor Otto III and Pope Sylvester II, possibly in collusion with Emperor Constantine VII, fabricated the Anno Domini dating system to place themselves at the year AD 1000 to legitimize Otto's claim to the empire. There was an almost three-hundred-year period in which Illig claims history was fabricated, including forging of documentation and creating of evidence. The time period, which includes the famous historical figure of Charlemagne, was e 297 years between AD 614 and AD 911. The basis of Illig's theory included the following principles:

- the lack of archaeological evidence from that period that could be reliably dated, and the overreliance on written sources of medieval history from this period;
- the presence of Roman architecture in twentieth-century Western Europe, which Illig suggests if proof that the Roman era was not as far back as we thought;
- the differences presented between the Julian calendar and the more newly introduced Gregorian calendar. The Julian calendar had a discrepancy of about thirteen days between it and the real tropical calendar year. The Gregorian calendar only adjusted for ten of those days, from which Illig concludes that roughly three centuries never existed.

Illig's theory has been debunked by fellow historians based on a number of points, mainly that Charlemagne did in fact exist, the Tang dynasty in China was in power during this purported missing three hundred years, and Halley's Comet sightings are reported and consistent with current astronomy with no phantom time added. The reason for bringing attention to this theory is not that I believe that there are three hundred missing years, but because I believe that leaders in the past could have had the opportunity to skew the truth about history. As the saying goes, history is written by the winners. The real question is, why would anyone want to add three hundred years to a "known" history? And if not three hundred years, what other information could have been rewritten for various reasons?

Khemitians

Another example of lost knowledge goes back to the ancient Egyptians, or rather the ancient "Khemit". In earlier chapters I have gone over the ancient archaeological feats, both in architecture and mechanical nature, that we cannot understand. But evidence shows that a sophisticated civilization lived in Khemit (the area we know today as Egypt) between ten thousand and sixty-five thousand years or more ago whose level of connection to nature and self-awareness allowed them to develop devices and advanced technologies that confound us today. The ancient borders of Khemit stretched much farther than the borders of the Egypt we know today, reaching deep into Africa, Mesopotamia, and the Mediterranean. The Khemitians used more than three hundred and sixty natural senses and were capable of energy work, manifestation, alchemy, and some believe transdimensional travelling. It is speculated that they had no need of a written or oral language, using higher brain functioning levels than we can today. Their connection with the natural environment and cosmos reached levels that we cannot begin to comprehend. The natural processes of water, energy fields, and awareness were open books to these ancients.

They combined the natural energies of the earth with sacred geometry to create structures that reflected the cosmology to mathematical perfection. They were not primitive by any means, but rather built structures that marked, amplified, and utilized the natural ley lines of the work in elaborate and complex manners. They used massive blocks of stone, each for its own energetic properties: granite, basalt, diorite, alabaster, etc. Pyramids were bio-organic energy devices that used crystal and frequencies of sound and water to generate vast electromagnetic energy fields. We cannot imagine with our current five senses the use of the higher-dimensional sensibilities that they must have employed. Some claim use of a sixth sense, but this is a far cry from three hundred and sixty.

New World Discoveries

Even United States history has been rewritten in recent years. We were taught that Christopher Columbus "discovered" the New World in 1492. However, we now know that Norse colonization of North America began in the late tenth century, when Norsemen patrolled the Atlantic. They settled in Greenland for almost five hundred years, and even the North American mainland in Newfoundland. There is evidence of unknown settlements even earlier than this. There are ancient burial grounds and copper mines all along the shores of Lake Superior which date back many years before the Vikings.

Figuring out who mined the copper, and where it went, has been the basis for much speculation. It is argued that perhaps the estimated 1.5 billion pounds of copper mined from the region was the source of the European

Bronze Age copper supply. The age starts in 3200 BC and spans the entire second millennium BC until approximately 600 BC. Near Peterborough, Ontario, there is a large stone which appears to be carved with a pre-runic alphabet that some suggest is ancient Norse. Could ancient Europeans have used North America for their mines, stretching as far west as the Rocky Mountains, north to the Arctic, and south to Louisiana? More cases of ancient ruins from many different time periods are being found across North America. It is theorized that the Knights Templar had knowledge of North America and that even Leonardo da Vinci knew of its existence. On top of that, as we have seen in previous chapters, there was evidence of world travel and exchange of information that defies our comprehension based on the history books.

Intentionally Destroyed Learning

Not only have we lost knowledge, but also there are many specific cases where it has been intentionally destroyed. Even in antiquity we find examples of mass book burnings: in the Bible King Jehoiakim burned a scroll written by the Hebrew prophet Jeremiah; Plato burned the writings of Democritus; and Alexander the Great destroyed Zoroastrian scriptures and the Persian Royal Archives. The Library of Alexandria was destroyed in part by the Romans, and the rest by order of Caliph Omar. The Temple of Jerusalem was razed along with the collection of knowledge there. The Book of Wisdom was destroyed by Inca ruler Pacacuti IV. Many times in our history, books and scrolls which contained ideas that were considered heretical by those perpetrating the destruction have been eliminated. The destruction of the House of Wisdom by the Mongols is one such example. The House of Wisdom was a huge library in Baghdad with the largest selection of books in the world about science, art, and Greek literature. It was ravaged by the grandson of Genghis Khan with the intent to wipe out Islam. Every religion has had its opposition and has seen the destruction of its collection of knowledge. These are just the known cases. As a species we do not take well to differences of opinion, race, or religion. Those who have failed to fit our model of what is right have been persecuted and conquered.

Even early Braille books were burned in Paris during the Industrial Revolution as being works of the Devil.

Voynich Manuscript

One manuscript which has survived and is the source of much controversy is the Voynich manuscript, handwritten on vellum which was carbon-dated to the early fifteenth century. The unusual thing about the codex is that it is in an unknown writing system with a highly regular structure to the words. The words are practically all between two to ten letters with few repetitions in the labels attached to the illustrations. The illustrations themselves are divided into six sections by scholars, with each being classified by style and supposed subject matter.

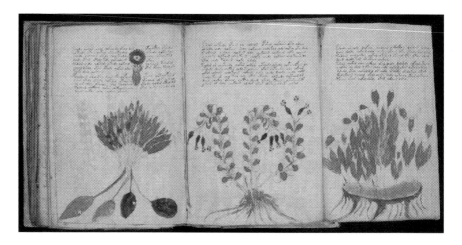

These sections are Herbal (112 folios), Astronomical (21 folios), Biological (20 folios), Cosmological (13 folios), Pharmaceutical (34 folios), and Recipes (22 folios). The subjects of the illustrations range from the mundane to the fantastical. The herbal section of the book fails to identify most of the plants with actual specimens we know today. Also, some botanists believe that the illustrations show flora from the New World. It would have been (according to our known history) impossible for the creator of the manuscript at the time to know what a sunflower was.

Another notable thing from the manuscript is the inclusion of what appears to be a dragon in one of the folios. The popular Western image of a dragon is of a winged four-legged creature that breathes fire. The earliest examples of dragons resemble giant snakes. Examples appear in the ancient Near East, ancient Mesopotamian art, Indo-Europe, and the Far East, including China and Japan. Some stories claim dragons bring luck, while others say they feast on humans. In Gambia, if you see Ninki Nanka, you will die within a few weeks. The Mester Snoor worm of Scotland would eat virgins for breakfast. Xiuhcoatl of Aztec mythology was associated with drought and the fire god Xiuhtecuhtli. In the Philippines, Minokawa gets blamed for eclipses; humans need to make as much noise as possible to keep Minokawa from swallowing the moon. In the Vedic region in early India, Vritra was a hoarder of the rains and brought drought. The Wawel dragon of Poland is the fire-breathing version we in the Western world associate with dragons. In Chile, a shape-shifting dragon called Peuchen is a huge flying snake that drinks the blood of animals. Beliefs may vary drastically by culture, but dragon-like creatures appear in virtually all cultures around the world. They are used in art, literature, architecture, and stories. Yet these creatures are considered myth. Why are there so many cultures that have such detailed information on these creatures, yet no evidence exists that they once lived?

The Anunnaki and Giants

Ancient Sumerian texts speak of the Anunnaki, descendants of An, who ruled the area and had humans dig gold for them. There are theories that the Anunnaki were a reptilian-like race, the "shining ones" who ruled Earth as gods. Was this species the origin of the draconic myths?

The children born of a mix between these gods and humans were said to be giants. The ancient hero Gilgamesh himself was said to be a half-god being of gigantic stature. There are several ancient texts, including the Bible, that describe giants. In Deuteronomy 3:11, Og is described as being "of the remnant of giants." He reigned in Mount Hermon (the area where Gilgamesh was also found). The Israelites were afraid to enter the land of Canaan. In Numbers 3:13, the scouts were cited as saying, "There we saw the Giant; and we were like grasshoppers in our own sight, and so we were in their sight." Of course, the most famous biblical reference to giants is the fight between David and Goliath. Was this just a metaphor, or was it from an actual confrontation? Pottery was found in the area with the name Goliath carved into it, dated from the same period as the story in the Bible. Perhaps there is truth to the existence of giant men.

At the turn of the twentieth century, several leading news publications at the time (including the *New York Times*, the *London Globe*, and *Scientific American*) published articles that giant human skeletons were found and their remains sent to the Smithsonian for further study. The evidence was never again seen or reported on, eliciting questions on whether this was a cover-up or if the remains were destroyed for some reason. There are many Native tribes that have tales passed down of white-faced giants who inhabited parts of what is now central USA. According to Paiute oral history, the Si-Te-Cah were a tribe of red-haired cannibalistic giants who lived in a cave. The tribe trapped the giants in the cave and set fire to the mouth, killing all within. The remains of between forty and fifty people were found in Lovelock Cave under four feet of guano. All the skeletons appeared normal, although large in stature at over seven feet tall. The skulls were preserved and taken to a local museum, where they are not on display. The skulls look normal, except the jawbones are unusually large when compared to regular human skulls, showing the proportionately larger size of these skulls. There have been rumours of skulls found in other places all over the world, along with picture evidence which is very quickly defamed as a hoax. While physical evidence remains tenuous at best, there is an endless trail that suggests giants, like dragons, once may have walked the earth.

Georgia Guidestones

In more recent history, there is the anomaly of the Georgia Guidestones. This set of granite slabs were erected in Elbert County, Georgia, USA, in 1980, by an unknown group fronted by a man going by a false name. The anonymity of the Guidestones' creators has made these stones a target for conspiracy theorists. Along with the inscribed messaging, there are several other features to the stones. The astronomic features include a hole drilled at an angle through the centre column to view the North Star; a carved slot carved is aligned with the solstices and equinoxes; an aperture in the capstone to capture the rays of the sun at noon each day, to indicate the day of the year; and the four outer stones that are oriented to the lunar declination cycle. Someone put a lot of thought into these features to preserve knowledge for posterity's sake. The question is, why would someone go to those lengths, ensure to have the message in several languages, and create rules for humanity that we are not living by today? There is also a time capsule, but no date is engraved as to when it should be opened.

The Guidestones are inscribed in eight different languages: English, Spanish, Hindi, Hebrew, Arabic, Swahili, Chinese, and Russian. In addition, the monument has Egyptian hieroglyphs and three other ancient language scripts, with shorter messages inscribed in the top of the structure. The monument is taller than Stonehenge, standing at nineteen feet three inches. The message carved into the stones contains a set of ten guidelines, one language being carved on the face of the four upright stones. At the top is inscribed, "Let these be guidestones to an age of reason." The body of the message is as follows:

1. Maintain humanity under five hundred million in balance with nature.
2. Guide reproduction wisely, improving fitness and diversity.

3. Unite humanity with a living new language.
4. Rule passion, faith, tradition, and all things with tempered reason.
5. Protect people and nations with fair laws and just courts.
6. Let all nations rule internally, resolving external disputes in a world court.
7. Avoid petty laws and useless officials.
8. Balance personal rights with social duties.
9. Prize truth, beauty, and love, seeking harmony with the infinite.
10. Be not a cancer on the earth. Leave room for nature.

Many have called for the destruction of the Guidestones, saying that the messages inscribed are satanic in origin. There is also the theory that the creators belonged to the New World Order and the Guidestones were a blueprint for global enslavement, calling for a culling by self-appointed elites who would use unknown means to exterminate most of the world's population. Why build something like this? Was this site meant to last beyond a possible nuclear war? Was it meant as a guide to rebuilding an already devastated civilization that was wiped out through war, plague, or other means? Is this act of preserving knowledge something other civilizations tried to do in the past but we no longer have the ability to understand what clues they left?

CHAPTER 5

Communication and the Cell Phone

COMMUNICATION IS OF UTMOST IMPORTANCE IN THE DEFINITION of what it means to be human. How we communicate with one another has evolved. Today, one of the most widely used methods of communication is the cell phone. Billions of people around the world are using cell phones. In fact, there are more cell phone subscribers in the United States than there are people, according to a study conducted by the CTIA (a trade association representing the wireless communications industry in the US) in 2011. I am sure it far surpasses those numbers today. Where the landline took place of some written communication when it became mainstream, letter writing was still an art and was the main form of contact over distances. The cell phone, however, has drastically changed the way we communicate. Whereas once we wrote, now we text or email (mostly in short form as it is too difficult to remember spelling or to write out all those extra letters). Whereas once we had face-to-face interaction, now we hide behind screens. Eloquence and verbosity are no longer the social norm; we use text-speak and communicate via social media. Emoticons, emoji, and GIFs have replaced feelings and how we express ourselves, removing the need for words altogether.

The cell phone has moved very far beyond its initial purpose of verbally connecting people. Rather than allowing users to be more connected, studies are starting to show that cell phone use insulates people more than ever before. For some, communication with those who are not present takes precedence over people in the same room. Sometimes, even people in the same room choose to communicate electronically instead of verbally. What was once an organic process that occurred in a very vital and personal way has been redefined by the cell phone—the way by which humans build their relationships and determine social hierarchy. Interaction over social media has the ability to develop or destroy relationships. "Friends" are people you might never have met in real life, and dating is just a swipe away.

In an article posed for the Smithsonian's podcast *Sidedoor,* we learn that anthropologists are studying the relationship between trouble with teenagers and the cell phone. Every post on social media is a catalyst for restructuring the social environment, with apps having the ability to uproot status. There is a lack of ability now to have face-to-face interactions, and the anthropologists fear the cell phone may depersonalize humans altogether. While there is no doubt that the widespread use of mobile technology has made it easier to communicate with people on the other side of the world, the question remains as to whether our communication is better.

There have been numerous studies to discover how our use of smartphones is affecting the way we communicate. One of these tests, performed by Shalini Misra, a psychology professor at Virginia Tech, found that in-person conversations where one party pulled out a cell phone while talking were generally rated lower in satisfaction and as being less fulfilling than when smartphones were not present. Our constant urge to seek out new information and invest our time into what other people are posting has created a gap in our connection to the people around us. The researchers also reported that the presence of a phone affected conversations between good friends more negatively than it did those held between strangers. It is becoming the cultural norm to alienate those closest to us through our dependence on technology.

Back in the 1950s and 1960s, the television became a popular household item. It was normal for families to gather around the television for dinner, or afterwards for an evening of entertainment. Families could still interact with each other through a shared experience, but cell phone usage is different in that it demands mostly solitary usage. Our standards for communicating have decreased, and there is a lot of room for error in getting the correct message across. It is a common belief that 55 per cent of communication is body language, 38 per cent is the tone of voice, and only 7 per cent is the actual words that are spoken. With the use of the cell phone, we are taking away 93 per cent of our communication cues and having to try to connect with just 7 per cent. With this handicap, our imperfect communication gets even murkier as humans are emotional and sometimes unpredictable in their responses.

Many studies have been conducted to learn the effect of technology on our ability to communicate face to face since the rise of the cell phone and social media usage. As Andrew K. Przybylski and Neta Weinstein of the University of Essex wrote in their study in 2012, "Recent advancements in communication technology have enabled billions of people to connect more easily with people great distances away, yet little has been known about how the frequent presence of these devices in social settings influences face-to-face interactions." In two separate experiments, researchers found that our devices and constant connectedness have negative effects on closeness, conversation quality, and the feeling of connection when engaging in an exchange of meaningful topics. It will simply be too long before we can know if there are significant consequences for the development of social skills (social awkwardness, social anxiety, etc.) in the cyber generation to make corrections.

There is an argument that video call apps like FaceTime, Zoom, and Skype are a benefit to communication rather than a hindrance. I would agree, but I believe that this is an exception to, and not the rule of, cell phone usage. We are inundated with information, and it is becoming easier to get distracted. With the ability to communicate whenever and however we want, the important or difficult messages we are trying to convey can get lost in the shuffle. Cyberbullying and suicides are on the rise, with little monitoring in place. Technological detachment is becoming today's reality, creating a lack of meaningful interactions. ATMs and self-checkout options allow for even fewer social interactions than in the past. We can run a business, do our banking, and even maintain an "active" social and dating life without ever actually speaking to another person face to face. Doctors are meeting with patients over electronic devices to deliver news; classes are conducted via web posts; and identities are created and stolen every day.

We are stagnating our emotional abilities by rejecting personal contact in favour of electronic communication. Research has proven that babies who are not held and touched will stop growing and may even die if the situation lasts long enough. Physical contact is necessary for the brain to learn to connect human contact with pleasure. This association is a main foundation for developing empathy. Touch can ease pain, lift depression, and create lasting connections that are stronger than time. We are depending on technology to replace physical contact in our creating and maintaining of relationships. Technology impacts how individuals engage in interpersonal relationships and how they behave within those relationships, and is essentially redefining what it means to relate as humans. As the capabilities of technology increase, our dependency on technology increases. Innovations in technology have done wonders for the fields of business and science, and for medical advancements. Technological innovation has given people the ability to work remotely and stay connected while travelling, but this can be a burden for people who are no longer able to disconnect.

So what impact is technology, specifically smartphones and computer access, having on our kids? Psychologists are quickly learning how dangerous smartphones can be for teenage brains. Research has found that an eighth grader's risk for depression jumps 27 per cent when he or she frequently uses social media. Kids who use their phones for at least three hours a day are much more likely to be suicidal. And recent research has found that the teen suicide rate in the United States now eclipses the homicide rate, with smartphones as the driving force. Even the technology executives in Silicon Valley are limiting access to devices for their children. As far back as 2007, Bill Gates stated that he implemented a cap on screen time when his daughter started developing an unhealthy attachment to video games. He also did not let his kids get cell phones until they were at least fourteen years old. Today, the average age for a child to receive a cell phone is ten years old. Even Steve Jobs revealed that he prohibited his kids from using the iPad when it was first released and limited how much technology could be used in the home. These parents seem to grasp the addictive powers of our devices more than the general public do, even though the former often make a living by creating and investing in this technology.

The fact that the people who are developing technology and sending it out to the general consumer have a wariness for the possible negative impact that overuse of technology can have on our kids is something we should take note of. "On the scale between candy and crack cocaine, it's closer to crack cocaine," Chris Anderson, the former editor of *Wired* and founder of GeekDad.com, was quoted as saying in an interview. Studies demonstrate these concerns are valid. The neurotransmitter dopamine, responsible for our brain's pleasure centres, is released in the bloodstream in an addictive rush when we receive a text, a like on one of our posts, or an email. Psychologists are hired to create and test persuasive designs for gadgets to increase their addictive properties.

The founders of Microsoft and the CEO of Apple have long been cited as mentioning established rules in their homes of limiting screen time for their children. However, in the general population, we find more examples of using the screen (whether it be television, phone, or computer) as a babysitter and parental replacement for our children. An interesting juxtaposition is the increasing double standard in the educational system. For years technology was reserved for the private and wealthy school boards. The original concern was that students in middle- to lower-income school districts would not have access to technology and gain the skills needed in an advancing technological world. Now, the exact opposite worry is being raised, that children of poorer and middle-class parents will be raided by screens, while the elite will return to focusing on human interaction and toys that stimulate physical interactions. Simple wooden toys and play-based preschools are on the rise in richer neighbourhoods that understand the value of creating meaningful interactions.

Will our children, so reliant on technology and their cell phones, be able to manage a large-scale technological crisis? In March of 1989, a geomagnetic storm struck earth, causing a nine-hour outage of electricity in Quebec. The storm that caused this event was known as a coronal mass ejection

(CME), aka a solar flare. Substantial communications blackouts occurred with short-wave radio interference (thought to be caused by the Soviets, as this was during the Cold War). They lost control of some satellites in polar orbit for several hours. Weather satellites were interrupted, and the sensors on the space shuttle *Discovery* were showing high pressure readings in the fuel cells.

These problems went away once the solar storm subsided, but they were a wake-up call showing us how reliant we were on technology and how easy it was for nature to disrupt it. Technology has come a long way since 1989; now there are many more satellites in orbit around Earth. Since 1996, geomagnetic storms and solar flares have been monitored in a joint project between NASA and the European Space Agency (ESA). Because of concerns that utilities had no set protection standards for severe solar storms, standards were created requiring power grids to be upgraded to protect from solar storms and tested regularly.

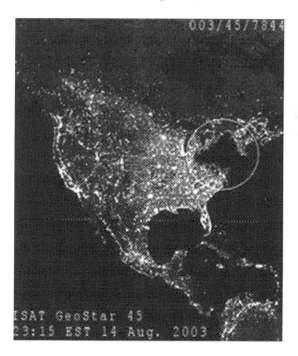

Much closer in our history was the north-east blackout of 2003, which affected an estimated ten million people in Ontario and forty-five million people in the USA. Most did not get power back for two days; in other areas it took as long as two weeks for power to be restored. The primary cause, we are told, was a software bug in the alarm system of the control room which overlooked the load on the transmission lines which drooped into trees as a result of being overloaded. If the general population were to find themselves out of power for a two-week period, anarchy and the collapse of society would occur. We are simply not equipped to handle life without technology, and none more so than our children who grew up relying on it.

CHAPTER 6

Covid-19 and Our Future

A S SEEN IN THE OUTBREAK OF THE CORONAVIRUS IN LATE 2019, early 2020, people panicked. There was a shortage of toilet paper, hand sanitizer, masks, and PPE for frontline workers. Many people were laid off, so governments had to step in with programmes to try to keep the economy stimulated. Hundreds of thousands of people were infected with the coronavirus, and tens of thousands died. Countries around the world closed their borders. Restrictions in many countries were militant with curfews and isolation becoming a requirement. Global supply chains were disrupted, international trade was curtailed, and tourism came to a screeching halt as the severity of the virus was continuing to compound. With forced lockdowns across Europe, Asia, and North America, the service sector and trade show industries were the first to be hit. The trickle effect continued until most people were working from home, with only a few able to continue daily activity as essential personnel. Imagine the increase in panic if the utilities were shut down, water and electric was no longer available, and there was no internet. The world would collapse.

So, what exactly is the coronavirus? There are several human coronavirus strains that are known to exist, including the coronavirus associated with SARS (severe acute respiratory syndrome)—SARS-CoV—and the virus named SARS-CoV-2, which is causing the current worldwide spread of the disease Covid-19. Coronaviruses are everywhere and are the second leading cause of the common cold (after rhinoviruses). The first coronavirus was isolated in 1937, causing illness in both humans and animals, but until recent decades it has rarely caused any disease more serious than a common cold in humans. The four major categories of coronavirus are known by the Greek letters *alpha, beta, delta,* and *gamma*. Only alpha and beta coronaviruses are known to infect humans. These viruses spread through the air and are responsible for about 10–30 per cent of colds worldwide. Long known to cause upper respiratory infections, coronaviruses were not felt to significantly cause pneumonia until relatively recently. A total of seven human coronaviruses (HCoVs) have now been identified: HCoV-229E, HCoV-OC43, HCoV-NL63, HCoV-HKU1, SARS-CoV (which causes severe acute respiratory syndrome), MERS-CoV (which causes Middle East respiratory syndrome), and now SARS-CoV-2. All but the 2019 Coronavirus version appear to be established human pathogens with worldwide distribution, causing upper and lower respiratory tract infections, especially in children, the elderly, and those at higher risk for infections. These respiratory infections can be quite serious.

Coronaviruses are zoonotic, meaning they can be transmitted between animals and people, but most infect only their specific animal host. It is rare that animal coronaviruses evolve to infect and spread among people, but this was the case with the severe acute respiratory syndrome coronavirus (SARS-CoV) and the Middle East respiratory syndrome coronavirus (MERS-CoV). SARS killed nearly 10 per cent of people who contracted it. MERS is even more deadly, claiming more than 30 per cent of people it infects. Unlike SARS, outbreaks of MERS still occur, generally spreading between people who are in close contact, which results in many fatalities of healthcare workers.

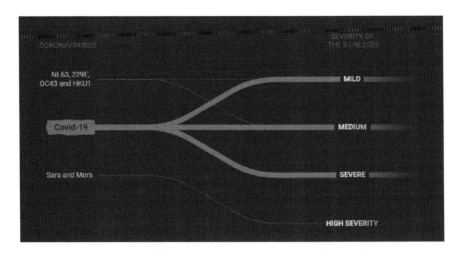

To date, there are still a variety of human diseases with unknown aetiology, including some of the coronaviruses. The SARS-CoV genome sequence is different from all other known coronaviruses, and it was first transmitted from civet cats to humans, though bats were determined to be the transmitter. Scientists also determined that MERS-CoV spread from camels to humans. The viruses in the *Coronaviridae* family, as the genus is known, are enveloped viruses with a large plus-strand RNA genome. They are named so because they look like halos (known as coronas) when viewed under an electron microscope. The viruses mutate and change at a high rate and have an unusual replication process. The replicase gene encodes a series of enzymes that use the rest of the genome as a template to produce a set of smaller, overlapping messenger RNA molecules, which are then translated into the structural proteins which are the building blocks of new viral particles. This is part of what makes this virus so deadly and so difficult to develop a vaccine for.

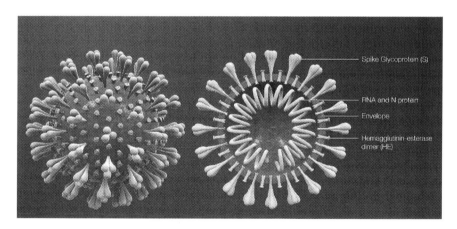

According to the World Health Organization (WHO), the most common symptoms of Covid-19 are fever, tiredness, and dry cough. Some patients may have aches and pains, nasal congestion, runny nose, sore throat, or diarrhoea. These symptoms are usually mild and begin gradually. Some people become infected but do not develop any symptoms, and most recover without needing any special treatment. The risk of catching the virus from someone without symptoms is low; however, the long incubation period means great opportunity for infection when someone is still asymptomatic. About one out of every six people who gets Covid-19 becomes seriously ill and develops difficulty breathing. Older people, and those with underlying medical problems such as high blood pressure, heart disease, or diabetes, are more likely to develop serious illness.

Viruses work by getting inside the cells your body is made of and then hijacking them. A virus first infects the cells lining your throat, airways, and lungs, creating huge numbers of new viruses that go on to infect yet more cells. The dry cough is the result of irritation as cells become infected. Your immune system releases cytokines to fight the virus, causing the body aches, pain, and fever. The disease can progress into a pneumonia-like cough and inflammation caused by fighting off the virus. The virus triggers an imbalance in the immune response, causing too much inflammation, and this is where it turns deadly. The tiny air sacs in your lungs fill with water, causing shortness of breath and difficulty breathing. In people with already compromised immune systems, lung disease, or cancer, this can be extremely dangerous. It is estimated that around 6 per cent of the cases turn serious. The problem is that the virus causes the immune system to spiral out of control, causing damage throughout the body. It can lead to septic shock when the blood pressure drops to dangerously low levels and organs stop working properly or else fail completely.

Acute respiratory distress syndrome caused by widespread inflammation in the lungs stops the body from getting enough of the oxygen it needs to survive. This can stop the kidneys from cleaning the blood and damage the lining of the intestines. Treatment at this stage is highly invasive, involving respirators and removal of the blood to try to oxygenate it outside the body. Damage done to the organs reaches a point where they can no longer keep the body alive. We are told by the CDC and WHO that the virus is passed from person to person through small droplets from the nose and mouth when an infected person coughs or exhales. These droplets can live on surfaces for days and are transmitted then through touch. Reducing the spread boils down to simple hygienic precautions: regularly and thoroughly cleaning hands with soap and water or alcohol-based hand sanitizers, maintaining a distance of two metres between individuals, avoiding touching your face, and staying quarantined at home unless absolutely required to go out. The people with the highest risk are typically getting the virus from people who may not even know they are infected. Men are more susceptible than women to the virus, perhaps because they are more likely to smoke, more likely not to wash their hands as much, or have a higher exposure to toxins in their jobs. This Covid-19 is more dangerous than SARS (which is actually more deadly) because of the period of time someone may be a carrier without symptoms. This evolution of viruses is definitely a concern. Scientists use bats to try to track the development of new viruses as bats can host viruses without being affected. Mutations between species occur when multiple animal viruses get crossed (e.g. H1N1). That is why there is concern with the live food markets in China. It allows direct contact between humans and other living species that would not normally be in close quarters together.

There has been a lot of speculation as to the cause of this virus; conspiracy theorists look at Donald Trump, China, 5G towers, big business, etc., all in an attempt to explain the widespread effects. One major aspect that has been examined with the spread is that a virus is not technically considered a living organism. Viruses require living host cells to duplicate and spread. Viral activity becomes prominent when the body has a high level of toxicity (which can be caused by pollution, chemicals, nutritional deficiencies, etc.). Viruses almost never dissolve living tissue, unless in specific circumstances such as polio and degenerative nervous system diseases where metal toxicity is present. Their primary function is to dissolve dead matter. They are very specific protein structures that are sequenced by blood cells via RNA/DNA. With some viruses, the only way to get a sample apart from natural means is through direct injection (vaccine) or blood transfusions with the virus in the blood. A perfect example of this is the human immunodeficiency virus, the virus that causes AIDS. HIV is unique when compared to most viruses because it attacks the immune system. The immune system gives our bodies the ability to fight infections. HIV finds and destroys a type of white blood cell in our bodies that our immune system must have to fight disease. HIV-1 is transmitted by sexual contact across mucosal surfaces, by maternal–infant exposure, and by percutaneous inoculation. One of the challenges people have with vaccinations is the level of toxic chemicals they also contain (see chart below). If viruses can only spread when there is toxicity in the environment and the immune system is weakened, are we not creating more of a problem by introducing some of these directly into our bloodstream?

Flu Shot Ingredients

Can you spot the disinfectants?

Influenza (Afluria) Quadrivalent	12/2019	sodium chloride, monobasic sodium phosphate, dibasic sodium phosphate, monobasic potassium phosphate, potassium chloride, calcium chloride, sodium taurodeoxycholate, ovalbumin, sucrose, neomycin sulfate, polymyxin B, beta-propiolactone, hydrocortisone, thimerosal (multi-dose vials)
Influenza (Fluad)	4/2019	squalene, polysorbate 80, sorbitan trioleate, sodium citrate dehydrate, citric acid monohydrate, neomycin, kanamycin, barium, hydrocortisone, egg proteins, cetyltrimethylammonium bromide (CTAB), formaldehyde
Influenza (Fluarix) Quadrivalent	©2019	octoxynol-10, TRITON X-100, α-tocopheryl hydrogen succinate, polysorbate 80 (Tween 80), hydrocortisone, gentamicin sulfate, ovalbumin, formaldehyde, sodium deoxycholate, sodium phosphate-buffered isotonic sodium chloride
Influenza (Flublok) Quadrivalent	4/2019	sodium chloride, monobasic sodium phosphate, dibasic sodium phosphate, polysorbate 20 (Tween 20), baculovirus and *Spodoptera frugiperda* cell proteins, baculovirus and cellular DNA, Triton X-100
Influenza (Flucelvax) Quadrivalent	8/2019	Madin Darby Canine Kidney (MDCK) cell protein, phosphate buffered saline, protein other than HA, MDCK cell DNA, polysorbate 80, cetyltrimethylammonium bromide, and β-propiolactone, Thimerosal (multi-dose vials)
Influenza (Flulaval) Quadrivalent	2/2020*	ovalbumin, formaldehyde, sodium deoxycholate, α-tocopheryl hydrogen succinate, polysorbate 80, thimerosal (multi-dose vials), phosphate-buffered saline solution
Influenza (Fluzone) Quadrivalent	2019	formaldehyde, egg protein, octylphenol ethoxylate, Triton X-100, sodium phosphate-buffered isotonic sodium chloride solution, thimerosal (multi-dose vials)
Influenza (Fluzone) High Dose	1/2019	egg protein, octylphenol ethoxylate, Triton X-100, sodium phosphate-buffered isotonic sodium chloride solution, formaldehyde
Influenza (FluMist) Quadrivalent	8/2019	monosodium glutamate, hydrolyzed porcine gelatin, arginine, sucrose, dibasic potassium phosphate, monobasic potassium phosphate, ovalbumin, gentamicin sulfate, ethylenediaminetetraacetic acid (EDTA)

Source: CDC
https://www.cdc.gov/vaccines/pubs/pinkbook/downloads/
appendices/b/excipient-table-2.pdf50

LivingWhole.org

Throughout the year, with seasonal and temperature changes, the body will dump massive amounts of toxins into the blood for removal. Some of these toxins are mercury or formaldehyde, or other chemical by-products that living microbes cannot feed upon. Nonliving proteins (viruses) are then manufactured by each cell in areas where the cleansing is necessary. The toxic substances are then broken down so the body can eliminate them. The only way a virus can be used as a biological weapon is through injection or mass inhalation. One theory is that chemtrails filled with aluminium particles, barium, strontium, and other heavy metals have been released through various means to settle on our crops, where they are ingested by animals and contaminate the water sources. Heavy metal toxicity is also investigated as having links to autism. Higher levels of heavy metals in our bodies mean higher chances of infection while our immune system is trying to flush these out.

On a global scale, people are bombarded with speculation about how this virus will impact the economy. On 11 March 2020, the WHO declared

Covid-19 a pandemic, creating a trickle effect of panic, cancellations, and economic disruption. Millions of cases have been confirmed worldwide; almost every country has been affected; and hundreds of thousands of people have died. The United States quickly outpaced every other country, with New York City being the epicentre for the outbreak. Italy, Spain, France, and the UK all recorded high levels of the outbreak and moved quickly to full lockdown quarantine for their residents. It took three months to reach the first hundred thousand cases, but it took less than a week for the number of cases to double from five hundred thousand to more than one million.

There is no doubt that the outbreak is currently having a major economic impact, with figures of unemployment surging to a record high. In the United States, President Trump was focused on the economy, but he learned he must wait out the continuing surge of cases along with the rest of the world. Just how detrimental could the coronavirus-induced recession be? It has been suggested that the economic downturn could end up killing more people than the actual virus. Some economists are saying it could boost overall life expectancy, with the virus weeding out those with weakened immune systems. The number of deaths attributed to the coronavirus could significantly increase if you factor in the financial fallout from the virus-containment measures that have shut down entire sectors of the economy and caused millions of people to be out of work.

After the recession of 2007–2009 due to the mortgage defaults in the United States, the trickle effect was felt around the world. While that was a major financial crisis, we are guessing at best on what the economic and health outcomes may be of this more recent crisis. When a country's wealth declines, its citizens may be exposed to greater health risks. We are getting a double whammy of the risks with the pandemic outbreak. It is difficult to extrapolate the current future trends based on past data. It looks like we could be heading into a severe global recession with production and innovation currently stalled. If you look at it from the idea of inertia, you see that it is much easier to keep an economy moving that is currently already on the move. Jump-starting one that is grinding to a halt may take a lot more effort. Many governments are trying to fight the halt by implementing emergency funding and support for people who are currently out of work. Major corporations are giving breaks on payments, loans, mortgages, and credit.

However, during a recession (and especially now with people quarantined in their homes), there can be surprising benefits. Pollution is declining, work hours are declining, and people have more time for themselves and their loved ones. Traffic deaths are on the decline as people are not on the roads. Also, people have more time to exercise and engage in self-care. So paradoxically, perhaps, a sizeable portion of the population may experience health improvements, both physical and mentally. Historical studies from the 1960s to 2010 have shown that the mortality rates in both the United States and the United Kingdom, where the studies were conducted, declined 0.5 per cent for every 1 per cent increase in unemployment. Who dies could depend on their economic role. Many people who lose their jobs and savings cannot recover from that. This is one factor which may contribute to a rise in suicide rates, even as deaths from other causes may decline.

The effects of the pandemic may be longer-lasting than we can imagine at this point. With big shifts happening in stock markets, many pensions and personal savings may be decimated. The markets have all seen massive declines since the beginning of the outbreak. According to Bloomberg, the Nikkei, Dow Jones, and FTSE all took a massive loss of up to 35 per cent.

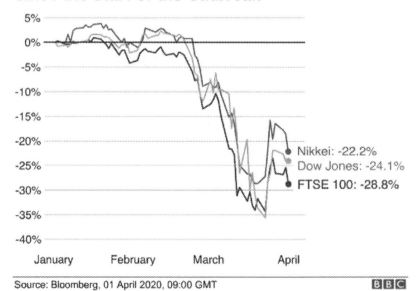

The impact of coronavirus on stock markets since the start of the outbreak

Nikkei: -22.2%
Dow Jones: -24.1%
FTSE 100: -28.8%

Source: Bloomberg, 01 April 2020, 09:00 GMT

BBC

Investors fear that the spread of the virus and government action to stimulate the economy is causing the downward drive in the markets. In response, banks have slashed interest rates, which in theory should encourage spending by making money more affordable. The market will continue to fluctuate as some sectors are still being impacted. One of the hardest-hit sectors was the travel industry. With more than one hundred countries implementing travel bans, tourism was decimated. Airlines cut flights as travellers cancelled trips for business and holidays. Some countries only allowed the crossing of its borders for citizens repatriating from abroad.

Supermarkets and online food delivery services saw a massive spike in their demand as customers rushed to stockpile toilet paper, frozen foods, and nonperishable canned goods. However, the food service industry was another sector that was hit hard. Restaurants could no longer open their doors to customers, and those with no online presence were immediately in danger of being closed for good. Global conferences and trade shows were cancelled, sports venues were closed, and any meetings of more than five people were banned in most countries. Schools were closed. Churches of all denominations were closed. The film and television industry stopped all production. Cinemas were closed. Retail that was not considered essential was forced to shut down. China faced factory closings, and as China does a third of the manufacturing globally, it will be a long time before restrictions placed on the supply chain are able to be mitigated. Car manufacturers found their sales grinding to a halt, and likewise oil prices have dropped to levels not seen in decades. In other areas, price gouging was driven by panic buying and disruption to the supply chains. Essential medicines were no longer readily available; electronic equipment was no longer being produced. The global GDP is set to stagnate, with the slowest rate of increase being caused by the outbreak. People looking for someone to blame held political leaders in contempt for their lack of control over the pandemic.

What will be the lasting impact of the global pandemic? What will the new normal look like? There is already a trend of working from home as companies implement and expand telecommuting technology usage. The question of whether there will be a negative impact on business travel and international conferencing as everyone continues with a virtual business strategy remains to be answered. With supply chains disrupted and the world's reliance on the Chinese economy in peril, will the impact of Chinese manufacturing forever change? Will we see increased restrictions on immigration; will closed borders be a way of life? There is no doubt that there has already been a major impact on relations between countries with the fear of the spread of the pandemic.

Are we going to go back to being comfortable in society, desperately wanting to go back to the way things were before the pandemic? Our lives have been altered, our behaviours have changed, and our loved ones have died. The busiest cities in the world have seen decreases in pollution. Animals have come back into places they had not been seen in years. But we have also seen a healthcare system that cannot provide basic protective equipment for its frontline workers; businesses that do not have enough cash to pay their rent or workers; and a government that has so severely damaged the credibility of our media that people don't know who to listen to for basic facts that can save their lives. The planet is healing while we are locked away.

What industries will prosper as an outcome to the pandemic? What will be the effect on the common person, and will we even recognize it? This is our chance to define a new version of normal, but will we take it? With the increased reliance on technology to keep us connected, will we continue to use technology to enhance isolation with fear governing our contacts? Is this a trap to get us to relinquish even more control over our daily lives, thinking it is easier to be told what to do and when? This disease has jumped us years into the future by increasing our reliance on technology, media, and the government. Never before have we, on a global scale, relinquished control of our day-to-day lives with such ease. Was this done on purpose? In Italy, one of the countries that was hardest hit, there was a massive shortage of doctors and nurses to support patients. AI robot doctors were introduced to visit patients. This practice is becoming more commonplace as AI is introduced into our lives. What will this increased dependence on AI mean for humanity? Is humanity in the slow process of dying out and being replaced? If so, what will be left behind? Is there a possibility that we have been here before and just do not know it? What about other planets? Are the mistakes we are making today the same process others have gone through—and it left them and their planets decimated? Could this be the urge that is behind the SpaceX programme and others desiring to sustain life off this planet? What do they know that we do not, and would we even be told?

CHAPTER 7

Technology and AI

Back in 2014, physicist Stephen Hawking and visionary Elon Musk were quoted as publicly addressing concerns about the future of AI. They agreed that there could be many benefits for humanity, but they also cited that AI could be the end of humanity if we are not careful. Hawking and Musk sat on a scientific advisory board, along with dozens of other experts, that works to "mitigate existential risks facing humanity". They drafted an open letter in 2015, first directed to others in the AI research field, then made public, calling for concrete research on how to prevent potential pitfalls in AI. The letter acknowledged the potential to eradicate disease or poverty but cautioned not to create something that cannot be controlled. It called for us to be proactive about banning offensive autonomous weaponry on a global scale.

Hawking knew that humans, who are limited by slow biological evolution, couldn't compete and would be superseded. He felt the emergence of artificial intelligence could be the worst event in the history of our civilization. While the potential is high for artificial intelligence being able to assist humans (he pointed out the potential to help undo damage done to the natural world), every aspect of our society will be transformed. Hawking was an early supporter of communication and other scientific technologies (for obvious reasons). His preference, however, was not to update the technology for his personal use. He insisted he did not want a more natural voice, that his robotic-sounding computer had become his trademark. Hawking also spoke about the benefits and dangers of the internet. He worried that it could become a command centre for terrorists and that more needed to be done to counter the threat. But what if the terrorist were the internet? AI would have the ability to take off on its own, and redesign itself at an ever-increasing rate. Would this intelligence decide that humans were a detriment to both it and the environment that needed to be eradicated?

A short-term concern is that, like during the Industrial Revolution, machines will become capable of undertaking tasks currently fulfilled by humans, thereby eradicating millions of jobs. As for longer-term concerns, people like Elon Musk warn that AI is our biggest threat. A few years ago, AI computers could not distinguish between a dog and a cat; now they can. They are still a far cry from a powerful, self-evolving software that Musk is warning about. Companies such as Facebook use AI for targeted advertising, photo tagging, and specialized news feeds. Microsoft, Google, and Apple use AI to power their digital assistants. The purpose of all these small steps is to get us closer to a self-learning AI.

Musk explained at a conference, in conversation with Demis Hassabis (partner in DeepMind, a company developing AI), that his ultimate goal with SpaceX was to create the ability for interplanetary colonization. He stated that humanity needs to have a bolthole in case of a disaster, or artificial intelligence going rogue and turning on humanity. Hassabis joked that AI would simply follow us. One of Hassabis's partners stated that he thought human extinction will probably occur and that technology will likely play a part in this. The question is, what part? Perfectly good intentions can still create something dangerous by accident. Musk stated at the World Government Summit in Dubai that scientists can become so engrossed in their work that they do not realize the ramifications of what they are doing until it is too late. As was the case with Dr Frankenstein and his monster, once you give a thing life, it decides what direction its life will take.

Unlike the slow interface currently existing between humans and computers, relying on finger movement upon the keys or speech recorders, the future may be a merger of biology and AI, a direct connection between the data in your brain sent wirelessly to a device, or even directly to a cloud-like computer.

This cyborg-like humanity is only a few years away according to some scientists. Musk plans to fight the unbridled delving into the world of

AI. He founded OpenAI, a billion-dollar nonprofit company working for safer artificial intelligence. OpenAI's mission is to ensure AI benefits all humanity. The company is attempting to build safe AI itself as well as assisting others to achieve this outcome. The concern is the lack of existing protocols and precautions. So far, public policy on AI is undetermined and the software is largely unregulated. In the United States, the Federal Aviation Administration oversees policy on drones and other unmanned flying vehicles, the Securities and Exchange Commission oversees automated financial trading, and the Department of Transportation is responsible for self-driving cars/trucks. Musk and his team at OpenAI feel that this is playing with fire. Fire may keep you warm, but it can also burn. So, what choices do we have moving forward? The list of things humans can do better than computers is continually getting smaller, but we created computers for just this purpose. We wanted to extend our reach and abilities beyond the human level.

Self-Driving Vehicles

There are several scenarios that Elon Musk has laid out in terms of future AI development. Some are positive; some are negative. The first of these is in relation to self-driving vehicles—the vehicle would automatically take you where you want to go. Safe roadways are a topic that gets a lot of attention in the public policy sphere. Fatalities from traffic incidents are increasing, many of them being preventable with an alarming number the result of distracted driving. With self-driving vehicles, there are no opportunities for distracted driving, and computers use complicated algorithms to determine appropriate stopping distances, distance to travel between vehicles, and other data to decrease the chance of accidents dramatically. This would also help to clear up congestion, along with many other fringe benefits (police would not have to ticket for speeding; autonomous parking; savings with decreases on car insurance; etc.). Some argue that the cost of this technology would be prohibitive to most and that the possibility for breaches in security is too high. This would be one additional area where we would lose a skill set that has become obsolete— and driving for fun would be relegated to special off-road areas only. In addition to self-driving vehicles, Musk feels that flying cars are not too far in the future either.

Self-Destruction

As our technology and our dependence on machines both grow, we risk making ourselves redundant in several fields. The loss of human jobs to computers is one thing, but Musk also fears that the global arms race for AI will cause another world war. The global competition to be the country with the most sophisticated AI could cause massive friction in an already unstable world environment. There is also the threat that the governments that lag behind will demand corporations to turn over their AI technology at gunpoint. But, worse than that, Musk posted the warning with a photo of a poster that reads, "In the end, the machines will win." AI will be either the best or worst thing for humanity—and we will not know until it is too late which it will turn out to be.

Digisexuality

One trend that is already starting to take off is coined "digisexuality". To engage in digisexuality is to have a relationship with something through artificial intelligence, whether it be online only or through an AI-driven robot. This trend has come quickly on the heels of growing worldwide acceptance of people who practise an alternative sexuality, including gay, transsexual, and bisexual individuals. The idea is that flesh-and-blood humans can forge fulfilling emotional relationships, or even sexual ones, with a digital service. Online avatars are taking the place of real people in relationships. In isolating societies like those in large cities or places like Japan, an online relationship with an avatar is becoming the answer for more and more men (as well as women). This idea is no longer confined to fiction movies but is being played out in real life. There are relationship robots programmed with an AI-equipped brain which allows the doll to communicate, remember favourite things, respond with lifelike expressions, and even simulate climax (but only if required by the owner). Some even have swappable faces to allow the "owners" to fulfil fantasies of multiple conquests.

The creators of these robots say they are designed to provide companionship as much as sex. For those who cannot afford the price tag for a personal robot, there are brothels popping up in places around the world to allow for sexual experiences with artificial intelligence. Some theorists believe that in the future the term *digisexual* will be more relevant than ever, with subsequent generations not caring about the difference between their online and offline lives. But is this kind of relationship in any way fulfilling? Is this really considered love? Will these digisexual relationships help real-life romance blossom, or will we, in pursuing them, replace the imperfection of human relationships with the ability to sculpt that which we define as a perfect relationship? In a report on the future of dating by Imperial College Business School and eHarmony, it was suggested that AI machine learning will be hugely influential in relationships of the future, whether this be from the online matches made for singles based on statistics and genetic code or from domestic digital assistants like Alexa who could intervene and complete an acoustic analysis of a couple's verbal communication to suggest improvements and resolution tactics. What about the possibility of cyberhackers and all your private data being downloaded from your "loved one"? There are also a number of moral, ethical, and legal questions that arise from the discussion which will need to be resolved concerning ownership and the power dynamics in a relationship between a human and a robot: Can a machine have free will? Does a machine have a right to choose its relationships? Is love a uniquely human experience? Is it something programmed into you? Would these new ways of experiencing love take away from our humanity? How will these interactions affect our emotions and other relationships in the long run?

Engineering Humans

CRISPR sequencing, a process for genetic engineering, and another morally debatable technique, stood out as Chinese researcher Dr He Jiankui used CRISPR-Cas9 to alter the DNA of a child in utero who would have been born HIV-positive. Although the United States at present bans quality altering, and although a considerable number of researchers have reproved Jiankui on moral grounds, defenders of the innovation wonder about its guarantee to one day destroy illness through and through, as we specially craft our descendants' properties as unequivocally as we select symbol attributes in computer games. Likewise, artificial intelligence is opening the entryway for the kinds of hereditary designing achievements that, at last, will permit us to develop our own progeny in remarkable ways. Utilizing AI, we will have the option to see how genotypes map onto phenotypes. We are going to be in a situation to comprehend what the specific qualities are for producing strong physiology and smarter minds and to create them at will. And beyond developing ourselves, we will design our world to suit our requirements.

But will this be the case? Or will AI grow to the point where it decides that humans and our needs are redundant?

AI advances are not merely changing the future of our homes, ourselves, and our lives; they are also edging their way into various businesses, disturbing the work environment. Artificial intelligence can improve profitability, effectiveness, and precision over human workers, but is this valuable? Many who dread that the ascent of AI will prompt machines and robots to supplant human specialists view this movement in innovation as a danger.

With the race for AI continuing, organizations need to understand that self-learning and self-discovery capacities are not an irrelevant part of a support structure in the workplace.

As there is expanding proof exhibiting the advantages of artificial intelligence frameworks, more leaders in the meeting room are looking more to what AI can offer their companies. Numerous organizations and people are idealistic that this AI-driven move in the work environment will bring about a more significant number of occupations being made than lost. As we create inventive advances, AI will positively affect our economy by producing jobs that require the specific range of abilities to work with the new AI systems. Computerized decision-making could be favourable when determining outcomes on a numbers or strictly financial basis, where the human element does not enter the process.

So, what will the near future of AI look like for us? The first thing we will see are progressively more skilled AI systems. Artificial intelligence will soon be able to emulate human discourse, decipher dialects, analyse vast amounts of information, and process it all in seconds. Secondly, we will see these frameworks become increasingly more present in our daily lives, even though we may not notice it. Thirdly, how we live will be way more controlled and driven by our online footprint. The information about our patterns, likes, and dislikes will be increased to such an extent that we no longer have to decide what to look for when shopping online, for example. It will be presented to us, and we will be told that based on previous purchases and activities, the new product or information will fit right into our lives. We see this with our Netflix accounts matching our tastes to new shows and with Facebook ads targeting us by our patterns. It will become much more encompassing.

This is one more example of our increased dependence on technology leading to devolution. We will no longer have to think about our likes and dislikes. The computers will decide for us what we should buy and when. We will be told our preferences in mates and will have the perfect match picked out for us, all by way of our digital footprint.

CHAPTER 8

AI vs Earth

A S AI DEVELOPS, IT WILL NOT JUST BE HUMANS WHO ARE affected by it. We have such an impact on our environment that any changes we make will have consequences for all other interconnected species on the planet. With the development of quantum computers and advanced AI technology, what happens when an impersonal look at numbers and calculated outcomes decides that humanity needs to be culled? What if a decision based on charts and graphs decides the planet needs a purge? With the trends in healthcare relying more on advancements than human interaction (for example robot doctors and WebMD), technology must create a stronger means of taking care of humanity. Dependency on our technology for our very health will be undeniable.

So, what are the top killers in the world from a medical standpoint? More than half the deaths worldwide are attributed to a top 10 list of causes, according to the World Health Organization. Ischaemic heart disease and stroke are the world's biggest killers, remaining the leading causes of death globally for more than fifteen years. Chronic obstructive pulmonary disease claims approximately 3.0 million lives per year, while lung cancer (along with trachea and bronchus cancers) causes 1.7 million deaths. Diabetes killed 1.6 million people in 2016, increasing sharply from less than 1 million in just a few short years. Deaths due to dementia more than doubled, making it the fifth-leading cause of global deaths with drastic inclines in a short time as well.

Respiratory infections remained the deadliest communicable disease, causing 3.0 million deaths worldwide and getting higher with new viruses such as SARS CoV-2 (which causes Covid-19), SARS, and MERS. The death rate from diarrhoeal diseases decreased by almost 1 million over the last few decades but still caused 1.4 million deaths. Similarly, the number of tuberculosis deaths decreased during the same period, but TB is still among the top 10 causes with a death toll of 1.3 million. HIV/AIDS is no longer among the world's top 10 causes of death with vaccines and awareness for prevention of the spread, along with new treatments that have been implemented to manage the disease. Road injuries round out the top 10, with almost 75 per cent of the fatalities being male.

Top 10 global causes of deaths, 2000

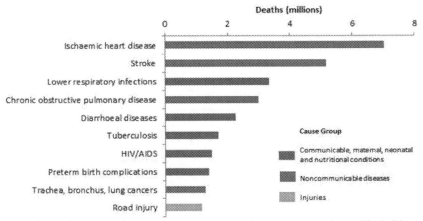

Source: Global Health Estimates 2016: Deaths by Cause, Age, Sex, by Country and by Region, 2000-2016. Geneva, World Health Organization; 2018.

More than half of all deaths in low-income countries were the result of the conditions depicted above in red, which include communicable diseases, maternal causes, nutritional defects, and conditions arising from pregnancy and childbirth. Lower respiratory infections were among the leading cause of death across all income groups. So, removing injuries from the list, as well as neonatal and nutritional conditions, we see that most of the top killers in the world have immune deficiencies in common.

Historically, we have had many cases where a "plague" or pandemic has wiped out a large portion of humanity. Looking back through history, let us examine some of these:

1. The Plague of Justinian

An influential Byzantine emperor in his own right, Justinian's reign is overshadowed by the outbreak of the first well-documented plague. It was believed to have originated in Africa, from there spreading to Europe through infected rats on merchant ships. It reached Constantinople in AD 541 and claimed up to ten thousand lives on a daily basis. There were so many dead that there were unburied bodies stacked in buildings or left out in the open. This caused even more spreading of sickness, killing over a third of the population. The victims of this outbreak had many of the same signs of the bubonic plague, including sudden fever and swollen lymph nodes. Even after it subsided in Byzantium, the plague continued to reappear in Europe, Africa, and Asia for several years. At least twenty-five million people were killed, but the actual death toll may have been much higher as proper records were not able to be kept as they are today.

2. The Black Death

In 1347 the plague invaded Europe from the East, thought to have been brought by sailors. The Black Death rampaged across countries for years with whole populations being wiped out. With little understanding of the cause, medieval physicians tried to combat the disease using bloodletting, lancing, and other crude techniques. It finally subsided around 1353, but not before it killed as many as fifty million people, more than half the population of Europe at that time. One silver lining was that the labour shortage caused by the disease was actually a positive for lower-class workers, who saw increased economic and social mobility.

3. The Italian Plague of 1629–31

The plague continued to surface and had a great impact on cities in Italy such as Verona, Milan, Venice, and Florence. In Milan and Venice, with lessons learned from previous outbreaks, quarantining was put in effect with the sick being shut in their homes and possessions and clothing being burned to prevent the spread of infection. The Venetians even banished some of their plague victims to nearby islands, away from the main population. The quarantining measures may have helped in preventing the spread (their version of social distancing), but the plague still killed more than two hundred and eighty thousand people, including over half the residents of Verona. Venice, meanwhile, lost nearly a third of its population of one hundred and forty thousand, which led to a decline in its ability to act as a city of power and influence.

4. The Great Plague of London

London, known for its cramped and filthy conditions, was hit by plague several times during the sixteenth and seventeenth centuries, most famously between 1665 and 1666. At its peak, as many as eight thousand people were dying each week. The wealthy isolated themselves in the countryside, leaving the city for the poor as the plague's main victims. As the sickness spread, city officials attempted quarantining, marking the homes of the victims with a red cross. Somewhere between seventy-five thousand and one hundred thousand people died before the outbreak subsided.

5. The Great Plague of Marseille

Ship travel was one of the top factors in the spread of the plague (like airline travel today), and this plague was no different. Travellers from the Middle East were infected when passengers were picked up with the illness. The ship was quarantined, but its owner convinced health officials to let him unload its cargo. Plague-carrying rats escaped with the cargo and spread across the city, sparking an epidemic. People died by the thousands. Convicts were used for disposing of the bodies. This plague lasted for two years, and it killed roughly one hundred thousand people.

6. The Third Plague Pandemic

The third major outbreak erupted in 1855 in the Chinese province of Yunnan, carried around the world by rats on steamships. This global pandemic eventually claimed fifteen million lives before dying out in the 1950s. Most cases were found in China and India, but there were also scattered cases from South Africa to San Francisco. The devastation on a global scale led to advancements in medicine and an understanding of the causes of the spread of these pandemics that we still refer to today. The graph below depicts the more recent outbreaks to help the reader visually understand the impact that diseases have had on global populations.

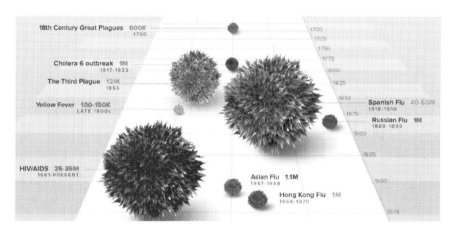

The people who are most vulnerable to these pandemics are people who already have compromised immune systems. As we have seen with the recent Covid-19 pandemic, it is the elderly and people with cancer, diabetes, heart disease, and/or a lung condition who are hardest hit. There is a very measurable demographic which equates to the highest costs to our healthcare system. Will those who are part of this demographic be the first to be eliminated in the culling of humanity? Like during the Black Death, does the elimination of the burden to our healthcare system allow the next generation to flourish without hindrance? As a purge which knocks out the greatest strain on the healthcare system globally, does it matter if this is a designer virus or naturally developed?

The rumour that Covid-19 was genetically engineered in a lab and released as part of a plot to depopulate the world persists. The way the virus is so targeted against the specific populations who are vulnerable and the two-week incubation period where the carrier shows no symptoms are the top reasons behind the theory. But what if the virus was just a naturally occurring mutation? What if the problem is not the virus itself, but the vaccines created to fight it? Two years ago, at a medical conference in Boston, Microsoft founder Bill Gates warned that the world wasn't prepared to handle a pandemic like that of the 1918 flu. "What the world needs—and what our safety, if not survival, demands—is a coordinated global approach. Specifically, we need better tools, an early detection system, and a global response system," Gates said. He predicted that the threat would not be the flu but more likely would be a new pathogen such as in the case of SARS and MERS. It is because of these types of statements and his involvement in the development of a vaccine for Covid-19 that theories of corrupt vaccines have arisen. There is the concern that microchips will be implanted with the vaccine, or that the vaccine is meant to cause sterility as a means of controlling the population explosion. Antivaccine activists claim Gates and his foundation are conducting global social and medical experiments via the World Health Organization. This is not the first time this type of accusation has been brought against the Gates Foundation either. In 2010, it was claimed that a project which was partially funded by the foundation had tested the contraceptive Depo-Provera on villagers in Ghana as part of an illicit population experiment. There is a long history of purported medical testing on different social and class structures: HIV introduction in Africa, medical sterilization of people of colour and in institutions, unsafe contraceptives, untreated syphilis, and many other events. The challenge with these theories, whether they have a kernel of truth or not, is their level of plausibility.

Human overpopulation is where there are too many people for the earth to sustain with food, water, air, and resources. The world's human population in 2020 was estimated at over seven and a half billion people, with an expectation of an increase to almost ten billion by 2040 if we continue at the same levels of growth as today. The range of estimated carrying capacity of the world is between four billion and nine billion, which means in many scenarios that we have already surpassed the level by several billion.

https://en.wikipedia.org/wiki/File:Popu

Overpopulation has severely impacted the environment with our vast requirements for resources and the amount of waste that we create. Species are going extinct to allow our population to expand, pollute, and clear-cut. Wild areas of the world are disappearing at rates that are inconceivable. Our impact on the oceans and pollution to the air is measurable, and yet incalculable. What if our developing AI decides that the planet needs a purge? What if it is the earth itself that decides that humanity needs to be controlled? Is Planet Earth the ultimate AI, or rather natural intelligence?

Let's look at examples of natural intelligence. The largest-known single-mass living entity is a colony of fungus in the Blue Mountains of north-eastern Oregon. This fungus, *Armillaria ostoyae*, which covers 2,384 acres of land, has one set of genetically identical cells that communicate with one another and coordinate their activities. The more we learn about plants on the planet, the more we see how much they are actually connected and in communication with each other. Even a forest of trees, each tree being a singular organism, is connected by a complex underground network called a mycorrhizal network, which can influence the survival, growth, and health of all the trees linked within it. The trees communicate and send resources where they are needed, with fungal threads acting as the go-between for the root systems.

Tree systems use the fungal network to transport nutrients. For example, a sapling that is unable to can't grow quickly enough because it is in the shade of a parent plant will receive nutrition from the larger plants through the network of fungal threads. They will even share resources between tree species depending on the season. Diseases that are lethal to trees can spread in a forest quickly, but tree systems will work together to prevent the spread. They have the ability to change their morphology and even biochemistry to combat toxins and pests, and a dying tree will even pass on extra resources to its neighbours to boost their ability to combat the disease. The many symbiotic relationships we see in nature and how the different systems work together should give us pause. We have lost touch with our ability to live in harmony with our world. We live in societies driven by economics and political gain instead of sharing resources and caring for one another. We are at a crossroads of choice. Do humans choose to evolve towards an AI platform with dependence on technology, or do we evolve back to a symbiotic living with the planet? Do we become part of the growth cycle, as opposed to being the virus on our planet? Do we even have that choice any more?

Nature is an incredibly strong force. Look at how quickly it takes over places we have abandoned. Within even five years, a place that once held humans will look like a forest again.

Trees will grow, and moss on a roof will absorb moisture and degrade materials like shingles. Windows blow out, and wind and rain get inside. Animals move in. Mould takes over everywhere. Concrete is broken apart by plant life. Metal is eroded. Moisture can split walls. There are thousands of examples of houses, churches, apartment buildings, and full cities that were built only a few short decades ago and now are abandoned and already reclaimed by nature. Looking at the materials we use for our construction, we find nothing to suggest harmony with the planet in a way that will last for thousands of years. If human life on the planet were to end today, what would be found as remains of our vast societies and cities? There would be more chance of finding ancient ruins still in existence than there would be of finding our giant skyscrapers. We are not creating a sustainable situation where we are in harmony with our environment. Will this be the doom of our species?

Our planet's core is molten, creating heat, energy, and life on the planet. Most of our science shows the sun as the source for energy on the planet, and this is true. But we forget about the energy that is generated directly by the earth itself. Geothermal energy is a process that is not widely used, mostly because of cost restrictions and lack of technology development because there is no profit in it for big business. The applicability, eco-friendliness, and potential for solving the global energy crisis is tempered by that fact. What if we were to get all our energy from the rotation of the earth? Magnetic energy is created by the earth; why not harness it? Our ancestors had access to alternative energy sources. Are these the technologies that we have lost? Because there is so much we do not understand, the earth technologies seem like magic to us. We can see evidence from ancient hieroglyphs that seems to show some form of technology or energy. Are these really just visual representations of different frequencies of energy that the ancients used?

Did they have a deeper understanding of certain waveforms and of shaping and using these forms for energy? Resonance and the restructuring of elements seem to have been key features to some of the abilities that we cannot grasp. Nikola Tesla developed a radiant energy source which would have given "free energy" to the world. His intent was to condense the energy trapped between the earth and upper atmosphere and transform it into electrical current. Electric power is present everywhere, if we only know how to harness it and use it. Tesla was shut down, but what if his is the path of getting back in tune with our world? If Earth is the ultimate natural intelligence, what else do we not even guess about the planet we are living on? What can we do to change our status as a virus to the earth?

CHAPTER 9
Conclusions

W E CANNOT KNOW WHAT THE FUTURE WILL BRING OR WHAT discoveries will be made in our lifetimes. There is so much that we don't know about our own past. Someone rewrote the history on us, and no one noticed. There are ancient engineering feats we cannot begin to comprehend today; ancient technology was readily available across the globe in ways we cannot understand. The Mayan calendar shows cycles of awareness and energy in relation to planetary alignment, showing we are at a low point in our abilities, not the peak of evolution as we believe. There is simply too much information missing in our history to explain the gaps in our knowledge. We know that humans have destroyed major caches of our own collection of knowledge, but why? Were we doing this of our own volition, or was someone trying to cover up things in our past that would affect our future? The cell phone is destroying our ability to communicate, to learn, and to function as we used to. Those who are developing the technologies that run our modern-day lives are the ones who are most concerned about the effects of said technology. Technology does not equal advancement of society, and many great minds warn against AI and its potential threat to humans. So where does this leave us?

We are simply not equipped to handle situations of global crisis, nor does our government want us to be. What is the level of human preparedness for a cataclysm of global scale? Why do we continually destroy ourselves with war, whether with weapons, chemicals, or technological warfare? Target-rich environments are the first to be destroyed. Is this what happened to ancient cities we are finding today? There is evidence in our past of mass destruction. There are flood stories in many historical accounts, not just found in the Christian Bible. Black stones have been found in Australia, France, India, Lebanon, South Africa, and Chile that contain aluminium and beryllium that have been exposed to high levels of radioactive bombardment and extreme temperatures. Where is the historical documentation of this event? Were the plagues that affected thousands of people across Europe and Asia caused by poor living conditions and rats, or was this early biological warfare with evidence of a strong-smelling miasma present before the sickness spread? There would be worldwide panic if technology were to fail—no water, no heat, no electricity, no food. The global economy would grind to a halt and there would be mass starvation.

We are not content to use technology only on our world either. We have been using radio waves in an attempt to locate and communicate with extraterrestrial beings for decades. Radio technology was used first and is only one of the types of communication techniques that have been utilized. What if our use of technology is inhibiting our ability to communicate? What if we had the ability to use a higher-level type of communication, such as telepathy or frequency communication (like dolphins use)? This idea of remote viewing, which is the practice of seeking impressions about an unseen target or event, has been labelled as a hoax by many, purporting that the use of extrasensory perception (ESP) has no basis in real science and is relegated to pseudoscience. With the declassification of the Stargate Project files back in the 1990s, a project sponsored by the US government as an attempt to determine potential military applications, the project gained a bit of popularity before it was established by various studies that there were no positive results. However, in a declassified document dated December 1986, there is a report compiled for suggested training procedures for remote viewing for the CIA. The conclusions and recommendations show that there was success in the process, and the suggestion is made that techniques should be developed to enhance the abilities we may have latently. Over the last three decades there must have been increasing breakthroughs along this line of thought, even if the studies have not been released at this time. Is this once again a situation where information has been presented to the public in such a way as to cloud the evidence?

There is a widely perpetuated myth that we humans use only 10 per cent of our brains, suggesting that a person may harness the unused potential and increase his or her abilities and awareness if only we could find the key to unlock the rest of our capacity. Changes to both grey and white matter following new experiences and learning have been shown, but it is not known exactly what those changes are. Physiological brain mapping shows all areas of the brain having specific functions, and nearly all areas are used all the time. What if this myth goes back to a time that could show that our abilities were curtailed on purpose, that we were given junk DNA to control our level of awareness and the length of our lifespan as is suggested in the Sumerian scrolls about the Annunaki? Are we able to somehow unlock and access higher levels of ability? What if the technologies we are using daily are creating an imbalance in our very beings and misaligning our frequencies, causing terminal illnesses of many kinds? There are many studies on how music improves memory and mood, but what if it's the specific frequency that makes the difference? Back in the early 1900s there was a push to standardize all instruments and orchestras to 440 Hz, different from the 432 Hz which is mathematically consistent with the fundamental electromagnetic beat of earth (8 Hz), better known as the Schumann resonance. If the two hemispheres of our brain are synchronized on an 8 Hz frequency, they work more harmoniously, with a maximum flow of information. It is also the frequency that is involved in the reproduction of DNA. The tuning of the worldwide frequency reference has no scientific relationship to the physical world. Playing, or listening to, music tuned at 432 Hz resonates with the organic world around you, creating a sense of peace and general well-being.

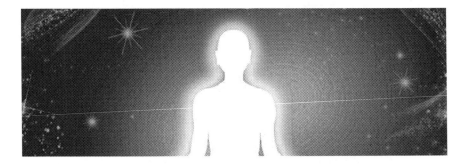

It is not known why the change occurred, but there is a theory that it was to use music as a way to control populations. Adherents to this theory point out that the 432 Hz can be connected to everything from the mathematical ratio of a nautilus shell to the construction of the pyramids. The conspiracy is that the Rockefeller Foundation and its leaders had an interest in ensuring the United States adopted the 440 Hz and in using this as a military weapon in the war on consciousness. This was to herd populations towards greater aggression, psychosocial agitation, physical illness, and financial impositions which profit the companies engaged in the upper echelons of control and finance.

This conspiracy may not be correct, or even only partially correct, but it is not the only reference to energy and frequencies that we should be aware of. One other is the study of ley lines, alignments demarcating earth energies upon which various historic structures are believed to be built. There are those who state that locations such as the pyramids and Stonehenge cause them to feel energy and positive frequencies. These places are supposed to crisscross the world and be sites of great power. One of the sites believed to be built on a ley line is the Great Pyramids at Giza. It is purported that the purpose of these was to create a free energy system for all people in the area through harnessing the sound and frequencies of the earth's core. This created a field of power using the building materials to either accentuate or carry the frequencies. Crystals were housed inside, and these vibrated to the frequencies carried by water. Any device requiring power was automatically powered if it was working on the same frequency. Nikola Tesla discovered that useful energy could be extracted and broadcasted to everyone in the world through the ground. His most famous attempt was his World Power System, using the Wardenclyffe Tower. His project was never completed, and he lost his funding from J. P. Morgan.

Even back then the elite would not allow free energy to be shared with the masses; there is no profit in free energy. There have been solutions developed to solve our dependency on fossil fuels, coal, and nuclear power. The patents have been bought at high prices and locked away. We live in a society of gender fluidity, the collapse of family, the rise of AI and the virtual world, unrest, mass migration from war-torn and underdeveloped countries, a rising drug crisis, and massive inequality in financial situations between the very rich and the poor. The pillars that define our society are beginning to teeter. Are we close to reaching the point of no return? In our history, the collapses have come when the elites pushed society towards instability by hoarding wealth and resources. The top 1 per cent earners of the world have more than 50 per cent of the world's wealth combined.

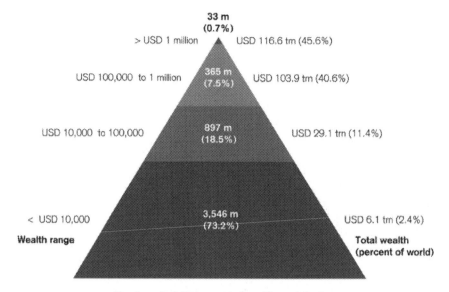

33 m
(0.7%)
> USD 1 million   USD 116.6 trn (45.6%)

USD 100,000 to 1 million   365 m
(7.5%)   USD 103.9 trn (40.6%)

USD 10,000 to 100,000   897 m
(18.5%)   USD 29.1 trn (11.4%)

< USD 10,000   3,546 m
(73.2%)   USD 6.1 trn (2.4%)

Wealth range   **Total wealth
(percent of world)**

Number of adults (percent of world population)

The answering of the questions of our origins as humans and whether we are alone or not has not been the purpose of *The Pandemic*. But the question remains, is there a cycle that is continuing of destruction, repopulation, development, then destruction? The history of our planet is *our* history. Are we allowing our history to be written for us? Are we allowing technology to take our places in the world? Is it inevitable that we will become nothing more than a digital footprint, an avatar, a number in the matrix? Is the triumph of humanity AI? Is the triumph of AI humanity?

RECOMMENDED READING

This is by no means a complete list, but following are books and articles I have found helpful:

The Law of One, Books I–V

Maharishi Effect, https://research.miu.edu/maharishi-effect/

Nichols, Preston B., and Peter Moon, *The Montauk Project: Experiments in Time*

Penre, Wes, *Dialogue with "Hidden Hand"*

Redfield, James, *The Celestine Prophecy: An Adventure*

Tellinger, Michael, *Slave Species of the Gods*

Tao Te Ching

Von Daniken, Erich von, *Chariots of the Gods? Unsolved Mysteries of the Past*